Coraggio!

Lessons for Living from an Italian Grandmother
The Course to Honor End of Life

By

Lisa K. Gigliotti, J.D.

www.WithCourageICan.com

Cover Design by Mary George
Front Cover Photo by Victoria Marchio www.vam-art.com

Printed in the United States of America

ISBN: 978-0-615-47368-0

Table of Contents

Coraggio!

Prologue

Coraggio! Lessons for Living from an Italian Grandmother
The Courage to Honor The End of Life

AT TWENTY-FIVE YEARS OF AGE I WAS LIVING LIFE FROM A WHEELCHAIR. Each morning of the two prior years, my prayer was, *God, please help me to walk. When my alarm clock rings, assist my legs to swing to the side of the bed that I may once more rise to my feet and take a step.* Instead, the first sense of morning awakening was screeching pain reporting from every fiery joint in my body.

To those heaven-bound pleas I added gratitude for my mother and my *Nagymama* (Hungarian grandmother) who housed me, fed me, and bathed me. My mother's positive spirit and melodious voice brought joy and optimism to my life. *Nagymama* strengthened my hope with her heavily-accented stories of flight from a high-society life, through a World War II-entrenched European continent, young daughters clutched against her undernourished figure. For two years they kept me physically alive, stoked the belief I would be cured of rheumatoid arthritis to walk again, and were my lifeline to the outside world. My spirit was undaunted.

On the eve of my Catholic faith's most holy night, the celebration of Christ's birth, I was slammed against the opposite—the reality of death. The voice of an anonymous emergency room volunteer haltingly declared that my mother had been killed in a horrifying car accident and that my *Nagymama* was being ushered to an operating room... not expected to live.

Comprehension of the words delivered by that compassionate voice became the most forceful karate-kick a young soul ever sustained. My previous bargaining with God for an ability to walk, now a seemingly trivial request, was quickly tossed aside in my entreaty for the news of the accident to be false. In its place I implored that the beloved women for whom I was dependent on for physical care, spiritual companionship, and maternal love would burst through the door in customary fashion: mom with a light-hearted song on her lips, and *Nagymama* with her native greeting, *Szervusz, Lillikem!* (Hello, my dear Lisa!)

In the immediate aftermath of the deadly wreck, there were obvious means to avoid grief's harshest agony: Mom's memorial service to plan, her eulogy to write, juggling of flights for my brothers and sister to attend the Los Angeles memorial service, phone interviews with the state police and coroner, conference calls with *Nagymama's* intensive care unit nurses, and arrangements to transport *Nagymama's* ashes to the family crypt in Debrecen, Hungary.

As weeks passed and the aftermath waned, there were fewer excuses to avoid dealing with the devastating grief. Yet I could not bear to allow my soul to go anywhere near the edge of feeling loss for fear my psyche would crack and subsequently shatter to pieces. *Bolster the emotional barrier lest you crumble into a weeping mess... unable to ever again partake in life.* I invested incredible amounts of energy to hold steadfast each day against feeling the pain, well-hid loneliness, and aching void. My fear of sensing the agony of that fierce blow stunted the process of grief.

That same year, when I was placed in a nursing home

due to muscle weakness and treatment for the newly diagnosed neuromuscular disease myasthenia gravis, it grew exponentially more difficult to evade feeling the emotion of loss. There was no telephone in my nursing home room and it was the pre-cellphone era. My nursing home roommate existed in a persistent vegetative state, unable to participate in a distracting conversation. The other residents failed to offer mental diversion due to the prevalence of dementia.

At night, when the nurses turned off my room lights and pulled closed the door, the mind tormentors could no longer be kept at bay. In the still and dark of that nursing room the tormentors would sneak through the weary cracks of my psyche's fortress. I had read the police report and coroner's report; scenes from the fatal car accident played across my mind. I knew what happened to my mother's body after being ejected from the car; the death certificate description of trauma listed as cause of death was photographically displayed in my mind. From an exhausted emotional state I tried to force away those haunting thoughts only to lose to a vividly detailed rerun. In a battle against the replays, I attempted to force a redo of the events leading to my mother's departure, hoping if I visualized a loving embrace and pictured myself saying, "Mom, I Love YOU!" the spoken sentiment would replace any cross word or action I had extended toward her.

From tortured mind and grief-besieged soul my cry was flung to the heavens with the last scrap of strength: *God, help me! I am slipping down a dark, slimy vortex and can no longer find foothold! Help me!*

In the still and dark of that nursing room night I heard a soft voice, a recollection of my Italian grandmother's voice, softly urging,

"Coraggio, Leeza. Coraggio."

My Italian grandmother (Nonna) had lovingly spoken the phrase to me on the day I was diagnosed with rheumatoid arthritis. On that day, I understood those Italian words to mean, *"Have courage, Lisa. Courage."* But I did not comprehend the power behind their meaning. Yet in the still and dark of that desperate nursing home evening the power of *coraggio* was revealed! Nonna's words and stories enlightened and empowered me! I thought about Nonna's Old Country stories…they told of adversity. I recognized that to these Old World figures hardship and death was a part of life…better said, hardship was a part of *living* life. Troubled times would appear, yet the figures in Nonna's stories did not shrink from a robust life in an attempt to avoid misfortune. Nor did they hide themselves after tragedy. They accepted their lot in life and made no excuses to avoid work, relationships, love, and celebration. At twenty five years old I came to know—in the still and dark of that nursing home night—that I had everything within I needed to survive.

From that night forward I used courage to propel me through legal education and career paths to become a disability advocate, a policy advisor to the Michigan Senate and to a governor, and currently as an administrative law judge. Courage fortified me for victory over physical challenges: aggressive immunosuppressive therapies, plasma pheresis blood dialysis, thoracic surgery to remove my thymus gland, four knee replacement surgeries, two ankle fusion surgeries, two ankle replacement surgeries, and an elbow replacement surgery.

I was a *testadura* (stubborn Southern Italian person), and combined with *coraggio* I could achieve career goals and overcome physical challenges. But what of my broken heart? I feared that even courage would not be able to heal the inner festering, roiling brew of grief.

There is an unspoken code in Italian culture: **honor**. Woven through the core principle of Italian life—to love with passion—honor creates a beautiful and resilient tapestry from which unfolds the lessons for moving through days in a masterpiece of cherishing and honoring the ones dear to us. That honor extends even after death. To the dear ones Italians loved passionately through life, honor is bestowed as passionately after death.

Italian women lost husbands and sons in wars or from accidents while laboring to feed their families. After their loss, these women donned themselves in black to demonstrate the honor they held for their loved ones. From the day my great-grandfather Genaro died from injuries sustained in a fall from the heights of his backyard pear tree, never once did I view great-grandmother Giuseppina except fully-clothed in black. It was effective. When entering the home of my great-grandmother, or my zii (aunts) in Italy, the black-clothed greeting was an instantaneous reminder to me of the fervent prayer they uttered each day for their beloved's soul:

Réquiem ætérnam dona ei Dómine;
et lux perpétua lúceat ei.
Requiéscat in pace.

Amen

(Eternal rest, grant unto him, O Lord,
and let perpetual light shine upon him.
May he rest in peace.

Amen.)

Ah yes...let perpetual light shine upon him; grief transformed daily into a beautifully meaningful love song.

In Old World Italy babies died during childbirth or within a few years. Lots of babies died. These Old World women did not shrink from the reality of death. They fully acknowledged their loss and openly shared their grief.

After Nonna came to the United States, the expressive acknowledgment of loss was shared via international mail; photo enclosed. Nonna would stand, hand-written letter in one hand, translating from Southern Italian dialect the malady or accident that had caused the death, while holding out to me with her other hand, the 3 x 3 square photo of a dead body. The dead body, most often a great-aunt or great-uncle, was stiffly laid in a bed in the same Southern Italian home he or she had lived... and died. Nonna returned the photo respect, and coaxed my siblings or me to bring our Instamatic camera to a funeral home that we could supply her with a dead-body-in-casket photo to mail back to her hometown. As I reached my latter teen years I wondered if the practice was morbidly odd. As I came to know more about the grieving process I realized it was not morose, rather, the viewing of a corpse was an important catalyst in the process of working through grief.

As tragedy propelled me into grief, so did tragedy present the opportunity for me to learn how to grieve the loss of my mother. As providence would have, I was staying with Nonna immediately prior to and following the shocking and tragic death of her only daughter. It was from Nonna's loud and openly demonstrative mourning for the loss of her beloved daughter that I witnessed a purging of tragedy's pain from the soul. From what at first was frightening to behold, I recognized a beautiful tribute to the depth with which she loved the child she birthed and devotedly cared for a lifetime. Nonna's courageous, head-on tackling of grief spurned the encouragement for me to face my own unresolved grief.

The experience was a springboard to healing grief with meaningful purpose. Before my eyes was a model for transforming grief into legacy. My Italian grandfather was known for gathering his children and grandchildren for the Sunday Italian Family Feast, and for his prolific garden which provided bounty for much of the Sunday Italian Family Feast. Nonna perpetuated my grandfather's legacy with a fierce determination to continue his garden and the Sunday Italian Family Feast as long as she was physically able. Nonna's example of transforming grief into legacy not only helped me identify the legacy I could perpetuate for my mother and *Nagymama*, it brought realization that each day was an opportunity for me to lay the groundwork for what might one day be my legacy.

From Nonna's Lesson Six comes the courage to experience grief, and spawn a healing from sorrow through honoring the legacy of a loved one. It speaks of Italian honor that extends beyond life on earth.

One gift to be derived from loss is the wisdom to live each day of your life as if it might be your last. Was your day spent in laughs shared and love exchanged? Did you build on the legacy you will leave behind? Part of my transformation from devastating grief to focus on creation of legacy was to start each morning by asking: *What imprint will I leave on a person's heart today? I pray my interaction lightens a person's heart.* And by aiming for a legacy of being joy, and light, and love for others, I hope that the moment my soul leaves its earthly body, God will look upon my radiant, smiling being and say, "Well done, my good and faithful servant."

Nonna's Lesson Seven illustrates life's greatest privilege: to honor others as they prepare to transition from this life into the next life. Honor and respect, two vital principles in Italian culture, are never diminished merely because old age or terminal illness necessitates dependence for hands-on care, and makes apparent the approach of death.

In current United States culture death is consciously or subconsciously feared, as youth and beauty are revered and pursued. Our proliferation of disposable items and over-scheduled, transient lives pave excuses for shuttling the aged to nursing homes, out of reminder's sight, and away from uncomfortable hands-on care and long-term, time-consuming attention.

A startling revelation about the difference between Nonna's Old World respect and honor bestowed at the end of life, and the current United States attitude came during one of our conversations. Nonna had received a photo of her Aunt Michelina, aged and infirm, in the bed of her daughter's home in Naples, Italy. As usual, our conversation was spoken mostly in English with occasional Italian words thrown in. Because I had never heard it before, I asked Nonna what was the Italian word or words for "nursing home." Nonna stared ahead silently, squeezing the velour-covered arms of her easy chair. After a moment she responded, "You know, Lisa. I really don't know what it is called, or if there is a name for it. In my town and your grandfather's town, there was no such thing as a nursing home. When a person got old or sick he lived in same home with his family. He might go live with his daughter if she moved to another home after getting married, but it was his son or daughter, or niece or nephew, that took care of him until he died.

Bam! It floored me to realize that in less than a century we had moved from embracing our dying with respect and love, to carting them away to avoid the bother or our fear of mortality. In Nonna's village and surrounding villages, there was no word to describe nursing homes because nursing homes did not exist. Nursing homes did not exist because family members considered it the most highly-honored privilege to care for a family member at the end of her life. An elderly family member lived in the same home, smelled the same foods being prepared, and heard the same children running throughout the house. The dying family member spent her last days propped up in the same bed she birthed her children, in the same bed she left this world, and in the same bed others would be drawn to pay their final respect.

This beautiful Old World devotion and recompense to the person who gave them life, or guided and loved them throughout life, continues to be respected. When visiting the homes of cousins close to me in age, in both Italy and Hungary, it is not unusual for them to point out the bed where their parent or grandparent took their final breath. Recently, I arrived at the family apartment of my sweet cousin Fruzsina Szentgyörgyvölgyi in Debrecen, Hungary. "This is the bedroom of Ili néni (my Aunt Ilonka, Fruzsi's grandmother and matriarch). Here the family grandfather clock stopped at the moment of her death. We have never tried to fix it. See, the clock's hands read forty-five minutes after twelve o'clock. The stopping of the clock at her last breath symbolizes something very important."

Love, Respect, and Honor; there is not a more important time to employ these values than when helping another being as he or she heads toward physical and spiritual transformation. There is no greater privilege in life than to provide human touch and compassionate words to a person struggling with the loss of physical dependence or resolving emotional issues in the years, months, or days preceding death.

As Nonna delighted in me, giggled with me, and was a fountain of love during formative years, so should I honor her at the end of her life by lending unselfish, dignified care, and spoiling her with unconditional love. Thus, the beautiful love story between grandmother and granddaughter would conclude with nothing less than a re-telling of life stories, reinvigorated giggles, unabashed hands-on care, and a total envelopment in love.

No one escapes death. That point was underscored in the production of this fourth *Coraggio* book. Three women who significantly contributed to breathing life into *Coraggio: The Courage to Honor the End of Life* had unexpected experiences of loss or encounters with terminal illness.

Karen Mysliwiec Pilat: my law school classmate with stage four breast cancer and "lesions on her to liver too numerous to count" helped edit the text. More significantly, Karen offered and wrote a chapter about an experience with which I had no personal encounter: the critical perspective of a person living with Stage IV cancer; death knocking at the doorstep.

Victoria Marchio: my gorgeous and spirited Italian cousin, artist, and photographer. When it was decided that the covers of books one, two and four would progress from the face of Nonna, to the face of my mother, and finally to mine, with Nonna's and my mother's in black and white to symbolize their passing from this earth, and mine in color to contrast my continued life, it was natural that Victoria would serve as photographer for a cover photo. Victoria and I needed to postpone the photo shoot on several occasions as her mother, my beloved Aunt Mary, was in the final stages of bladder cancer. It was Victoria who, in the months after her mother's death, shot the contemplative original cover photo outside of her Chicago home; with snow-covered barren tree branches symbolizing the winter season of our lives, and looking toward the afternoon winter sun; the radiant light that calls us home.

Mary George: the stroke of her graphic artist pen poured symbolism into the cover borders of all four *Coraggio* books. For this book Mary crafted a design using Nonna's favorite lavender flower and a heart, to signifythe story of a remarkable bond of love between a grandmother and granddaughter, found between the covers' borders (See Chapter 7, *Dorme Bene, Bella Nonna*). To accomplish the meaningful creations, Mary stole time away from tracheotomy suctioning and tube feeding her beloved John, after his unexpected cancer surgery and chemotherapy treatment.

Three courageous women. Three women who create legacy instead of folding to devastation—as they walk through each day honoring the end of life. *Coraggio! The Courage to Honor End of Life* is far from depressing or morose. Join as we heal grieving hearts and seek to be active participants in one of life's greatest privileges—so that you, too, may *"Dorme Bene!"*

CHAPTER 1

The Italian Death Wail

Brrriiiiing...brrriiiing.

Shrill tones jolt me semi-awake, jumbling my dreams, sending them scrambling. *Is that a ringing phone?*

Brrriiiiing...brrriiiing.

The ring sounds distant...but from where?

Brrriiiiing...

Why the continuing ring?!!

Irritation fluctuates with curiosity as I battle between the desire to ignore and the desire to problem-solve.

Brrriiiiing. Brrriiiing.

The harsh sound of the ring fades into darkness. In some fuzzy, back alley of my brain I become semi-aware that the darkness is a dream. The ringing hovers at the edge of my dream but I am pulled away from its aggravation into the warmth of much needed slumber.

Oh thank goodness for peace.

God knows I need sleep.

Oh please Lord...make the penetrating annoyance stay away so I can S-L-E-E-P!

Its sharp return rudely prods my consciousness into awakening and I realize that a phone actually is ringing. In that awakening state where the mind straddles between reality and dreamland I try to figure out where I am. Dawn is making an attempt and in its virgin light I can make out landmarks. My eyes focus first on the curves and post of an old mahogany footboard. Beyond the footboard looms an antique mahogany chest of drawers. With my conscious state returning I recognize the chest of drawers as Grandpa Francesco's.

Ah...right...Grandpa's room.

I am in Grandpa's bedroom, lying high above the floor in his half-century-old bed. From as far back as I can remember Nonna and Grandpa had separate bedrooms. Grandpa Francesco's bedroom remained with the same bed and dresser furniture as the day he died. And I was lying in his chestnut-toned, inlaid wood bed—the woodwork ornately handsome despite the occasional chipped or missing piece of inlay.

Details of my current situation return to me. I had spent the night at Nonna's. My third knee replacement was to occur this morning and my father was going to meet me at Nonna's and drive me the hour it took to travel to the University of Michigan Medical Center in Ann Arbor.

Uh oh! The determined phone caller was making another attempt! I fought with bedcovers as boldly as Prince Valiant slashed aside the thorned brambles to reach Sleeping Beauty, trying to hurriedly escape the weighty restraints to reach the phone in the living room. Heavy bedcovers are no easy feat for a person with arthritically sore and inflamed elbows. But as in the Sleeping Beauty fable, time was critical in my quest to reach the phone before the caller abandoned another futile attempt.

Who in heaven's name could be calling so early? It's not even 5:30 A.M.! What was so urgent?

Perplexed, I quick-limped to reach the phone as fast as was mechanically possible on my thoroughly deteriorated knee.

Oh thank goodness…whomever it is keeps letting the phone ring…they must know neither Nonna nor I hold the world's speed record for the phone dash!

With grogginess waning I deduced the caller was most likely my father regarding the ride to the hospital so I was not too surprised to hear his voice.

"Lisa?"

He was a "stick-to-the-original-plan" kind of guy so I knew some event had occurred important enough to change the plan.

"Where have you guys been?" His voice had urgency, almost irritation.

"I have been calling since three in the morning!"

The truth was Nonna and I had both been sleeping - which was exactly what we should have been doing during the middle of the night. Guilt-ridden as always I started making excuses to my father for why I had not awakened to his first calls. I had been pushing myself at work and home for the past three days to get caught up before the prolonged job absence needed for knee replacement recovery. I was exhausted and probably in a deep, fatigued sleep. There was also the problem of Nonna's snoring—loud enough to hear through the bedroom door. To buffer the blasts I had inserted earplugs and buried my head under Grandpa's overstuffed, feather pillow. Anyway, it was the middle of the night so what else but deep sleep was expected…?

"What is it Dad?'

No response. I tensed when I realized the long pause was caused by my father choking back his emotional sob. *Oh Lord. What has happened?*

"Dad…?"

"Your Aunt Connie is dead."

"What? How's that possible?" I continued stammering. Aunt Connie was Dad's younger sister and as far as we all knew she was feeling healthier than she had felt in years.

"Evidently it was a pulmonary embolism….She woke up saying she was having a difficult time breathing and wanted to go to the hospital. Uncle Bob put her in the car…" His voice cracked and broke off. "…but she probably died before he could get her there."

I sat in stunned disbelief. Seconds passed without a word uttered. It was in my immobilized state of shock that my father sadly and softly directed, "You need to tell Nonna."

"Nuh-huh. No way." As if it was not shocking enough to hear my aunt was dead, I could not bear to think of being the one to tell Nonna her only daughter was dead. To top it off, I was scheduled for major surgery in a few hours. *Oh, right. What about the surgery?*

My father and I very briefly debated whether to continue with the surgery as planned that morning. After weeks of preparation on the surgeon's part and on my part, should I abruptly cancel so I could be present to support my cousins with Aunt Connie's sudden death? The operating room team was probably already assembling and preparing for surgery. The surgeon was most likely already on his way to the hospital. My father firmly supported going ahead with the surgery. In order to pick me up and get me to the hospital in time for the early morning pre-operative prep he had to immediately jump in his car and pray that the international border crossing at the Detroit River tunnel connecting Windsor, Ontario with Detroit, Michigan was not delayed by U.S. Customs. He was right. It would have to be the one to tell Nonna.

Oh dear Lord. Why did you have to pick the night I spend at Nonna's for this to happen? Why me, Lord? I did not care if I sounded chicken-hearted in my query to God. I could not tolerate the thought of being the person to deliver the news to sweet, optimistic, little Nonna...that her only daughter was dead. On second thought, I recognized the selfishness of my rebuke to God. *I guess it was good you had a family member here because this news may be too much for her to bear.* I resigned myself to be message bearer. *Well then, Lord, you better help me think of what to say because I am bereft of any idea.*

The dozen-feet of hallway from Nonna's living room to her bedroom usually seemed unbearably long when traversing with pain-wracked knees and ankles. But the distance seemed all too short now and I arrived at her door with a mind completely void of a plan for delivery. She was asleep. I dimly turned on her bedside lamp, softly sat on the edge of the bed and gently touched her arm.

"Nonna?"

"What...*what?*" She slurred with a slight startle. "What *Leeza*?"

"That was Dad who just called. Did you hear the phone?" What an inane question. Of course she hadn't heard the phone.

"No, I did not hear the phone." She answered sounding sleep-grogged but in earnest even though it was a stupid question.

"Dad...he...had some really bad news..." The last couple of words were garbled by sobs. Nonna's almond shaped brown eyes were now large, round and black. I grabbed her hands and she grasped her hands over mine as I saw her struggle to fight the lump growing in her throat.

"Oh, Nonna...Oh, Nonna...It's bad...It's ***really*** bad..."

I wanted to tell her gently, calmly, with comforting words of wisdom. Instead, the whole story tumbled out in seconds, despite sobbing so hard words sputtered only two or three to a sequence. That is how Nonna learned that her only daughter - Concetta - had died. In the minutes that followed we held each other, sobbed, expressed disbelief, and continued to sob. She said she needed to use the bathroom. I watched her stand to make sure the shock had not made her physically unstable. Then I left her side and with gulping sobs rushed to prepare for my father's imminent arrival to take me the hospital.

It was then I heard it for the first time. **The Italian Death Wail!** That shriek–pulled from the depth of a besieged, grieving soul and then flung to the heavens in its tormented passion. You have heard the term "bone-chilling?" Well the sound of the first Italian death wail froze solid the inner marrow of my bones–instantly!

I pled for mercy. *Oh, God. Oh, dear God. Help us, dear God!*

And then I heard it again. That terrifying wail ripped into my heart and I am sure my heart would also have been flung out to the heavens but for the large lump that had expanded in my throat to block its path. It was Nonna. It had been less than a half of an hour, but the reality that death had occurred had sunk in. And now she had started grieving the loss of her only daughter. I did not know whether to stay away out of respect for her to employ this part of her mourning in private, or rush to her bedroom and embrace her where she stood. I just stood in place, stunned. Immobilized again for the second time in one hour.

The Italian death wail is not crying. It is not cursing or yelling. It is a high-pitched moan that ascends and descends octaves. The emotion carried along the howl could melt the coldest heart.

A few hours later I underwent my third total knee replacement surgery. I managed to get discharged from the hospital within a couple days–the shortest time possible for a total knee replacement patient–and returned directly to Nonna's home. I was in her kitchen, manning the phone, the newly replaced and securely plaster-casted knee propped on the vinyl seat of one of the 1960's-style kitchen chairs. From that makeshift command post I called Aunt Connie's son regarding her funeral and burial services in Alabama. Her son, my first-cousin, was a smart-as-they-come aerospace engineer from the aerospace mecca of Huntsville, Alabama. Although Nonna was in her bedroom at the other end of the house, my cousin could clearly hear The Italian Death Wail through the phone.

"I have to hang up," he said curtly. "I cannot bear to hear Nonna like that." He panicked and apologetically hung up the phone.

I did not feel the same as my cousin did about hearing Nonna grieve. I admit, the first time I heard her I felt as if I wanted to run as far away as I could from the sound of this old woman's pain. At each of the dozens of utterances in the days following, the sound sliced cleanly through my heart. But the sound of her despairing wails no longer had the effect of "run and avoid." Although it distressed my heart to hear Nonna's excruciating wail, in a strange way I admired her for having the courage to face all of her pain…the courage to face the totality of pain from her loss head-on…the guts to express that pain, her anger, the loss, with every bit of furor she desired. For her wail told the story of her love for her daughter, Concetta. Her pain was recognition of the love she had for her daughter—a child she bore, nurtured, and of whom she was proud. Her cries were for loss of the earthly mother and daughter bond of friendship. Nonna's wails were a demonstration for herself and for the heavens of that love and that loss. Her protestations were of a grave injustice: "No mother's child should predecease her. It is unnatural, *Leeza*."

I was never able to find the courage to grieve my significant losses as Nonna did. Provide advice on how to stumble through grief and make it to some better place? Not me. I stink at grief. With my mother's unexpected death I was so afraid of feeling the intensity of pain that might rush in the minute I allowed myself to feel the loss; I tried my hardest to block feeling the loss. I shoved it down. I was the fabled little Dutch boy who stuck his finger in the hole in the dike to prevent the force from gallons of powerful water behind it from destroying the entire wall. The problem with continuing to restrain grief…it consumed more and more energy to keep the anguish suppressed. It now took my whole body pressed against the dike to keep my finger in the hole against the force of water pushing for escape.

Stamping down the emotions of my agonizing loss was most likely unhealthy. In hindsight I believe that the strongly forced suppression was detrimental to my physical health and stifled healthy emotional growth. But what I learned is that allowing yourself to feel the pain and the loss as you grieve also draws forth the feelings of the love and joy you experienced with the person. My words sound simple. In reality it is not that simple. For me it helps to remember Nonna, The Italian Death Wail, and by her example muster the courage to feel loss and grief.

It takes courage:

- To face the ache of loss and grief.
- To overcome the fear of feeling the ache of loss and grief

CHAPTER 2

The Process Of Grieving

I STINK AT GRIEVING. IT IS DIFFICULT FOR ME TO TALK ABOUT GRIEVING EVEN now, no coincidence that the subject lands as the final *lezioni*, putting off until the end that subject which is most painful for me. I have so mishandled grief that I think it best to rely on the wisdom of others to explain the process of grieving.

At 17 years old my Grandpa Francesco's death was a traumatic period in my dramatic adolescent life: I had been separated from my mother for several years, was in teenage rebellion against my father, and the pivotal person I felt loved and accepted me, Grandpa Francesco, had just been torn from my life. Dominican High School teacher Sister Joan Weitz gave me Elizabeth Kubler-Ross' relatively new book, *On Death and Dying*. Sr. Joan asked me to read it and report back to the class what aspects I thought were helpful. Sr. Joan was one of the nuns we thought were "cool" in high school. I felt honored that she gave me this important responsibility. I knew that it might be a veiled attempt to help me through my loss, but did not care about the guise. Although Kubler-Ross' book title inferred it was about stages of dying, the author intended the stages to be applied to any catastrophic personal loss, such as grieving the death of a loved one. As I read her stages of dying, and grief, I was impressed at Kubler-Ross' ability to clarify the stages:

1. Denial and isolation – a shock response, "This is not happening to me!"
2. Anger – angry at God or others, "Why me?"
3. Bargaining – bargain with God, "If you let me live to do this, I will do that."
4. Depression – mourning for losses that have occurred or are yet to come.
5. Acceptance – accepting the fact that death is inevitable.

I wondered in my adolescent know-it-all disposition why some psychologist had not delineated and articulated the stages prior to this date. The stages seemed obvious to me. Nonetheless I was eager to report to my fellow students the important findings. I remember sitting cross-legged in a vinyl bean bag on the rust colored shag carpeting of Sr. Joan's small Senior Seminar "classroom." Dominican High School was "progressive" for a Catholic all girl high school in that school uniforms had been abandoned. But then again it was the 1970s. In classic 70s style, we sat nestled in a circle of bean bags, adorned in jean bib-overalls.

To the floor-lounging classmates I openly expressed some of my feelings about Grandpa Francesco's death that directly related to Kubler-Ross' stages of grief. I did not believe I had experienced all the stages and not in the order described by Kubler-Ross. Because I had not progressed exactly as described in the book, I worried with slight adolescent exaggeration whether I was psychologically fit.

When my mother and grandmother were killed in a car accident eight years later, I thought back on the Kubler-Ross' stages. I tried to identify what stage I was in at a given time, but felt as if I was stuck in one or two stages, never reaching several of the other stages. I grew concerned that something was wrong with me; I was not systematically moving through all of the stages of grief, neatly reaching closure for one stage of grief and stepping efficiently to the next.

I discovered over time that there was nothing wrong with me; rather I experienced grieving in waves. Instead of moving through grief packaged in pre-defined, sequential steps, grief crashed into me unsuspected, engulfed me in heartache, and then ebbed gently away. Grief's wave crested during times of association: a first birthday after the death, the first anniversary of the death, the first Christmas after the death, in every tear-jerking Mother's Day television commercial, in a bowl of Italian Wedding Soup, or in the scene of a movie. I have learned that it is better to allow myself to fully feel the emotion at peak times—to allow the wave to crash down over me—than to exert the energy needed to stiffen against the colliding sentiment. Yes, I shed a tear when the television screen shows a chubby-fingered little child proudly holding out a hand-picked, crumpled flower in gesture of pure, genuine love to his mother. *Yes. Even Jesus wept when he learned of the death of his beloved friend Lazarus.* But I am careful to not get stuck in the emotion; reminding me that grief is a process and with the moments of sadness or unfairness there will be moments where a memory brings a smile or a chuckle.

It takes courage:

- To recognize that your emotions of denial, anger, bargaining, depression, and acceptance may be stages of grief.
- To be kind to and patient with yourself as you work through the stages or waves of grief.
- To allow others to experience their stages of grief without judgment.

Chapter 3

Dreams and Apparitions as Grief Resolution

For almost two decades I have had a recurring dream. The theme of the dream is always the same. I find myself at some place. Unexpectedly, I meet my mother. My heart leaps with joy. The adrenaline starts pumping and I feel my throat closing. I am so relieved I almost start to cry. I exclaim a version of:

"Mom, I found you! They said you were dead, but I see you are alive!" Before another second is wasted I blurt out, "Thank God. I just wanted to tell you, "Thank you. Thank you! I never got to tell you how much I appreciated all the care you gave me while I was sick... all the duets you sang with me… all the _____"

Or "Thank God you are still alive! I needed to tell you I

am sorry for how unkind I was to you and I am sorry for not forgiving you."

Or "I knew you were alive, Mom!! Thanks heavens because I wanted to tell you in person how much I love you."

As I could feel myself being pulled awake from the dream, I would fight it tremendously.

"Please, please do not be a dream! Please be true! Please be happening! Don't be a cruel joke. Please Mom be alive!!"

But always I wake. My pillow is damp from my own tears. My body shakes with sobs, choked by the swelled feeling of my throat and twisted guts from the sick feeling of devastating loss. Can you say "Unresolved grief"?

My stepmother, Bonnie, is an amazing woman. Bonnie was a schoolteacher in a small town in southeast Ontario and the organist at her church for many years. Bonnie and I share in the sisterhood of "motherless-daughters," she losing her mother at 19 years old while in her first year of university, London, Ontario. As she describes it, she visited her "Mum" in the hospital while home from university. She recalls how in the 1970s the medical profession did not talk with a person about the fact that she had cancer or that she was dying of cancer. During the hospital visits with Mum the fact that Mum was dying of cancer was not discussed, and as a result, the end-of-life resolution of past grievances, present expressions of gratitude and love between mother and daughter were forgone. After her mother passed away, Bonnie was plagued with emotionally-charged nightmares. In many of the nightmares Bonnie found herself in face-to-face conversation with her mother, only to wake distraught but with no resolution. A well-recognized phenomenon, dreams may occur as the subconscious mind attempts to work through unresolved issues. In Bonnie's case, she was in essence in her teen years when her mother went through the dying process. She had been raised to respect her elders, including not speaking back. She was faced with her mother's death in an environment that attempted to hide the basic truth that death was imminent. As a consequence of all the factors, Bonnie was left with unresolved emotions after her mother died. Exasperated by the recurring nightmares Bonnie recognized she had to deal with the unresolved issues between her and her mother in order to work through this stage of grief. Bonnie knew what she had to do and prepared herself with prayer and emotional strength. In the next dream where her mother appeared, Bonnie spoke the truths she held within herself. They were truths about how she felt her mother had been wrong or too harsh, followed by the truths of daughterly love she needed to express. The dream was vividly real. The unresolved aspects of grief thus being resolved, the Mum nightmares ceased. Her mother was no longer in a physical form to work through unfinished mother-daughter business, yet Bonnie used dream-based interactions to bring peace to a difficult aspect of grief.

I have heard many, many stories about how a dead person appears to a loved one in heavy mourning and delivers great peace. I wonder to myself, was it truly an apparition, or did the person dream the entire event? Shortly after Nonna died, my father said he awoke in the middle of the night. After a brief visit to the restroom he returned to bed. He felt a presence at the end of the bed. The presence felt so strong that my father was compelled to ask out loud,

"How is my mother?"

The presence answered: "See for yourself!"

My father was perplexed at the seemingly smug answer. It was dark in his bedroom and his mother was buried a hundred miles away. How could he see anything? What was he supposed to be seeing there, in the middle of the night, in his bedroom? In the darkness images appeared in front of him. He saw gorgeous flowers, some resembling white daisies, their yellow centers one foot in diameter. As the flowers swayed gleefully in front of him the voice said:

"These are the flowers your mother grows now. As you can see, she is well and happy."

Oh, dear Nonna! In her later years she spent the majority of her spring, summer and fall days in her garden. There could never have been a more appropriate and accurate description of Nonna's well-being than to see the marvelous fruits of her heavenly efforts. My father shook himself to see if he was dreaming. No, he was awake, sitting up in his bed. He grasped the skin on his arm in a last attempt to determine if he was in a waking state. Yes, he saw the skin squeeze together and felt the pinch.

My father was moved to the extent he was rendered speechless about the event. He fervently wished to tell his wife Bonnie, but as he tried to begin, he felt his throat close and no words were released. After several attempts throughout the following days proved unsuccessful, Bonnie, in her calm reassuring way said,

"It is okay, Pat. When the story is ready to be told, you will be able to tell me."

My father was overwhelmed and grateful to know that not only was his mother okay, he had also been given a supernatural demonstration of her well-being. As the overwhelming emotions of peace and gratitude soothed the pain of his grief, my father was able to describe to Bonnie what had happened. It was more than a year before my father could describe the events to me and even then, the emotions of peace and gratitude were continued with such intensity his throat tightened several times and he had to pause before continuing.

Could Bonnie's mother have appeared to her even though Bonnie thought it a dream? Did my father truly gaze upon Nonna's heavenly garden? I do not know the answer to these questions and I am unsure if in my lifetime there will be conclusive evidence one way or the other. What I do know, is that Bonnie was aware enough and courageous enough to battle through the grief in her dreams. What I do know is that my father is courageous enough to believe in his apparition and thus reap the fruits of peace.

In a manner similar to my father I harvested peace, but the pivotal events for me were apparitions both Nonna and my mother told me about shortly before their deaths.

About two years before Nonna's passing I made my usual weekend trek from Lansing to her home in St. Clair Shores. No matter that I always packed my luggage the night before so that I could hit the eastbound trail directly from work; I never was able to arrive in Nonna's living room before 7 p.m. Even though I would hit the metro-Detroit traffic post-rush hour there never failed to be an accident or perhaps for no discernable reason, bumper-to-bumper traffic. After the long day at work, the long week at work, tiredness added to my impatience with sitting hostage in my car when, if every car could merely move along, I could be sitting in Nonna's kitchen eating the bowl of Italian Wedding Soup and baked butternut squash she had waiting for me. And so it was that I arrived on Friday night after 7 p.m.

Nonna was always excited and talkative when I arrived to spend the weekend with her. She sat in her velour recliner patiently and watched while I carried in my belongings and the cooler stuffed with specialty Italian treats I tried to spoil her with each week. The ritual continued such that when I finished unloading we would both head into the kitchen where she in turn would spoil me with a home cooked, love-packed, Italian snack.

As I made my third pack-mule plod from my car through her living room I noticed a postcard displayed on top of the phonograph console. It is important to understand that the top of the console was akin to a shrine. The special designation of holy ground was related to my grandfather (Nonno Francesco). In the mid-1960s he purchased a $33_{1/3}$ revolutions per minute (RPM) record player. The $33_{1/3}$ RPM record player was enshrined within a maple veneer console; the cabinet about four feet wide, its four short legs adding to its height of about $2_{1/2}$ feet above the taupe carpeted living room floor. The speakers at each end of the console's face were covered with a face of classic late 50s fabric: course brown yarn woven through beige and metallic gold threads. To the midpoint of the console face was a hidden compartment whose door slid aside to reveal Grandpa's record albums.

The console and record albums were Grandpa's prized possessions, second only to his wine-making instruments: imported European wine press, grape crusher and California oak barrels.

Grandpa played his Italian record albums over and over, singing with all the gusto he showed for life. I remember every falsetto vocal arrangement that made us pint-sized grandchildren giggle; each vocal impression of an instrument's sound that fascinated us. There were a couple of albums in particular he loved and in turn I also loved.

Primo were the melodramatic performances of the songs *Torno Sorrento* and *Oh Marie!* due to his passionate portrayal. My siblings and I sat mesmerized on the couch facing the console, the eight feet of floor between couch and console now his stage. Step aside Luciano Pavarotti! He, too, stored a white handkerchief in the deep, boundless pockets of his forest-green workmen pants. But unlike Pavarotti the handkerchief emerged from the hidden depths as my Grandfather sang the song *Mamma*. He was close to a three hundred pound gregarious man, but he cried at each rendition. He would start:

"Mamma, son tanto felice
Perché ritorno da te.
La mia canzone ti dice
ch'è il più bel sogno per me!"

But his mellow voice soon started cracking…stifling an all-out sob as he reached the climactic part:

"Mamma!
Ma la canzone mia più bella sei tu!
Sei tu la vita
E per la vita non ti lascio mai più!
Mamma… mai più!"

We knew what was coming. We knew he would not be able to finish. We knew the passionate bellows would be choked to a squelch as his eyes filled with tears. It was then that his white linen handkerchief would be retrieved from the baggy work pants pocket to dab the corner of his eyes.

Years later when I watched Pavarotti whisk a handkerchief in similar gesture I believed the international opera star merely copied the genuinely forlorn great tenor Francesco Gigliotti. Yet, even though we knew this large, robust Italian man was about to break down mid-song we sat there, elbows on our knees, palms holding our chins, staring. Unapologetically staring. We were kids. What did we know? Later, when we were in kitchen with Nonna and Grandpa was out of hearing range in the backyard garden Nonna would explain Grandpa's emotional display. She wiped her hands on the kitchen towel and bent closer to toward our faces so she could quietly explain. The song *Mamma* was about a man singing to his mother. The man bemoaned the distance from his mother, a continent apart in Italy, but remembered the closeness of his mother's love. In the sentiment of that memory the man sings of how he dearly he misses his mother and how he hopes to return to his mother. Nonna told us that Grandpa had left his mother in Italy to come to America when he was only a teenager, had not returned to see her again, and the separation made him sad.

But Grandpa's phonograph did not only bring gushy songs. From our couch perch we doubled over in laughter until Grandpa reached out his hand to grab ours, yanking us into the feet-stomping tarantella he had started. Or gesturing to stand next to him and imitate playing the musical instrument he mime-depicted while singing *Eh, Cumpari*. Grandpa had the corner on air guitar decades before charade instruments became the rage.

Grandpa bellowed the *Eh, Cumpari's* question command to us in a false vibrato:

"E comu si sona 'u vilulinu?" (And how does it sound—the violin?)

and we would extend our left arms straight out from the chin and move an invisible violin bow across the imaginary violin with our right hand to display to him how the violin was played.

Grandpa's next melodic command:

"E comu si sona a la trombona?" (And how does it sound—the trombone?)

and we would hold the imaginary trombone to our lips and use our right hand to move the sliding piece of the instrument to its proper note!

Grandpa would shift his massive weight on a heaved hop from one foot to the other during these happy songs until the vases and standing picture frames on top of the television console would start to rock and Nonna would call out to him from the kitchen "Gi!" in alarm.

I concur with the cliché about every Italian-born male being and opera star…I spent many childhood afternoons serenaded by grandpa's bellowed dramatic cantatas. I never knew there was an English version of the song *Love Is A Many Splendored Thing* until I was in my late teens!

Needless to say, Grandpa's $33_{1/3}$ RPM yielding Magnavox brought great joy and sentiment to his family and to him. His neighbors, who I am sure received unsolicited serenades, may argue to the contrary.

Grandpa's phonograph had gone unused, silenced after his boisterous singing presence passed from this world. Nonna did not even know how to use it. I remember opening the top once to show her how to gently lift the diamond-tipped arm and place it in the grooves of the shiny, black vinyl album, but she drew away, claiming she was afraid of breaking it. Yet Nonna would never consider getting rid of the phonograph console or Grandpa's collection of $33_{1/3}$ RPM black vinyl jewels. They stood as the Francesco Gigliotti monument.

That is how the top of the maple veneer console became hallowed ground. Thus any item placed within this hallowed ground had reached a place of importance and esteem in Nonna's consideration. And the items remained in specific order according to some hierarchical configuration derived by Nonna. There was the wallet-sized photo of her sister-in-law Carmella's young grandson Mario, who had died a decade ago in a tragic accident while swimming in the

Mediterranean ocean, just over the mountain from their home in Pedivigliano, Italy. There was another photo, no larger than Mario's, taken of Archdiocese of Detroit Adam Cardinal Maida, standing next to me at a 1999 Thank You Reception for all volunteers who worked to defeat the 1998 Michigan assisted suicide ballot proposal. A photo of her granddaughter, standing with the leader of the Catholic Church in Michigan, definitely ranked in the category of worthy for placement on top the console. Of course the *Capo di Monte* creamy-white porcelain basket filled to overflow with its characteristic various pastel porcelain flowers. *Capo di Monte* Italian artisans used extreme temperature kilns to form the thick but hollow porcelain figurines and flower baskets. *Capo di Monte* porcelain was imported from Italy or if you were lucky, one of your relatives would come from Italy and bring you one. Nonna's basket was an oval shape of about four inches long by three inches wide, its mound of flowers reaching about three inches in height. I would guess it cost approximately $35 dollars – a luxury to Nonna. Nonna had one *Capo di Monte*. It made her feel rich. She displayed it in its righteous place atop the console with an air of aristocracy.

But as I arrived this Friday night, displayed on the revered console was a new item. Protected within one of those clear Plexiglas frames was a mysterious yellowed card, precious enough to be granted a position of esteem on top the record player cabinet.

The appearance of this postcard was odd. It showed a handsome man, twenty years at most. It was a 1920's vintage post card, photographed in black and white, a skilled watercolorist had tinted the face a flesh tone and the thin lips a shade of pink too dark for a man. The standing man appeared slim in his late 1920's style suit, despite the boxy, notched lapel suit coat and baggy pants. I stared more closely at the face. Black hair slicked to a shine and pencil-thin mustache were emphasized by the flesh tone watercolor. The eyes were narrowly slit, and the large Italian nose was familiar...let me think...*very* familiar...oh yeah...just like mine. The same distinct Italian nose I had regretted my entire life.

I was standing, holding the plastic encased card close to my face now. Nonna was watching me. She knew my curiosity was about to burst but she offered no information. Nonna's happy chattering had clamped to a halt when my attention had turned to the postcard. Okay. It was going to take some delicate coaxing to get this story.

"Um, Nonna...who is this?" I had a pretty good idea who it was but I thought I would politely ask.

"It is a picture of your grandfather."

That was the entire answer. I stood holding the photo, not breaking my gaze upon it, and not responding in any manner so that Nonna could expound, but that was the only scrap Nonna offered.

"Wow, Nonna. He was really handsome." Silence on Nonna's end.

"How come it's a postcard? I mean...how come he had a picture made into a postcard and then mailed it to you?"

I guess it was the right question because Nonna gratefully gushed, "We were engaged. He had to go to Pennsylvania to look for work in the mines because there weren't no more good jobs left in Detroit. It was getting into the Depression days. I guess he missed me so he had this photo taken and, you know, they made it into a postcard in those days. He wrote his feelings for me." Nonna paused. She continued softly, "He...he wrote he loved me." Nonna paused again. Talking about the postcard was definitely stirring intense emotions.

"He sent it to me."

What? How could it be that I was forty years old and never before seen this photo? Not that I could recall seeing it anyway. I became caught up in my mind over this puzzling development. For many seconds I had totally disengaged from Nonna.

"*Leeza.* Your grandfather has been coming to me." Her

voice had brought me back to the reality of her small living room but the meaning of her words could certainly not be real. I am sure my mouth was open, but because no words were coming forth she continued.

"He comes to me…" she stopped, as if deciding whether to tell me the rest, "he comes to me and beckons me." I turned to look at her. Her face was somberly serious, her eyes focused straight ahead.

"When he comes to me…*Leeza*, when he comes to me… he looks just as he did in that photo."

Oh mama mia! The thick mass of Italian hairs on my arms was sticking straight up. I tried to remain calm and I surprised myself by the calm tone I used when I asked Nonna, "Do you mean you dream about Grandpa?"

"No. No *Leeza*. He came to me twice in my bedroom and appeared once here in the living room."

O Dio! It had happened more than once? Even during the day while she was awake?

Those eerie thoughts caused an icy chill to trickle through my body. I shuddered.

"Where did you get the postcard?" I was trying to make rational sense out of something that was sounding supernatural.

"It showed up when I was looking for something else. Out of the blue. I didn't even know I still had it. *Don't you see, Leeza*???

Nonna's voice became insistent, as if she thought I did not believe her.

"That is what I mean *Leeza*. ***He…keeps…coming…to me***."

Nonna did not act sheepishly, as if I thought her crazy. No. She was serious. There was a bit of sadness in her voice as well. I almost asked her if she knew what it meant but I stopped myself as my brain caught up to my lips and commanded them to remain shut. I did not say it. But at that moment I knew what she was thinking. And at that moment I knew, that she knew I knew, what she was thinking.

am sorry for how unkind I was to you and I am sorry for not forgiving you."

Or "I knew you were alive, Mom!! Thanks heavens because I wanted to tell you in person how much I love you."

As I could feel myself being pulled awake from the dream, I would fight it tremendously.

"Please, please do not be a dream! Please be true! Please be happening! Don't be a cruel joke. Please Mom be alive!!"

But always I wake. My pillow is damp from my own tears. My body shakes with sobs, choked by the swelled feeling of my throat and twisted guts from the sick feeling of devastating loss. Can you say "Unresolved grief"?

My stepmother, Bonnie, is an amazing woman. Bonnie was a schoolteacher in a small town in southeast Ontario and the organist at her church for many years. Bonnie and I share in the sisterhood of "motherless-daughters," she losing her mother at 19 years old while in her first year of university, London, Ontario. As she describes it, she visited her "Mum" in the hospital while home from university. She recalls how in the 1970s the medical profession did not talk with a person about the fact that she had cancer or that she was dying of cancer. During the hospital visits with Mum the fact that Mum was dying of cancer was not discussed, and as a result, the end-of-life resolution of past grievances, present expressions of gratitude and love between mother and daughter were forgone. After her mother passed away, Bonnie was plagued with emotionally-charged nightmares. In many of the nightmares Bonnie found herself in face-to-face conversation with her mother, only to wake distraught but with no resolution. A well-recognized phenomenon, dreams may occur as the subconscious mind attempts to work through unresolved issues. In Bonnie's case, she was in essence in her teen years when her mother went through the dying process. She had been raised to respect her elders, including not speaking back. She was faced with her mother's death in an environment that attempted to hide the basic truth that death was imminent. As a consequence of all vest, with braided gold trim and gold buttons. It was the kind of form-fitting vest with the white cotton puffy sleeved shirt. He had soft curls of light blond hair, similar to mine as a child…and when he turned to me…Lisa…he looked just like me…only he was a man…like the male version of me! When he looked at me, a strange sense warmed my whole body…I can only describe it as the most incredible closeness to a being I have ever felt before."

She paused now. She was kneeling on the floor at the side of my bed, her usual position for holding the morning carrot juice glass while I barely leaned forward from the bed pillows. She had leaned close to me this morning, to share this fantastic secret. So close to my face now I could smell the fragrance of her face moisturizer and feel the warmth… perhaps the warmth that had been passed from the beautiful, angelic, Hungarian young man. Although my mother had affection for California more than any land she knew, her soul had never truly left the motherland onto which she was born. If an angel was to appear to her it made sense to me that the angel would be a Hungarian angel. But there was much more to the story.

"Lisa…" She hesitated. "I think he was my twin soul."

"Whoa!" My mother and I talked often about her belief that there were twin souls in the universe. This was not the trendy "soul mate" of the new age genre, for example, "we both like the same things…tee hee hee …we're so compatible…gush, gush." No. Twin souls were spiritually connected at a higher level, almost a metaphysical level, at the risk of sounding new-agey myself. It was the concept that two souls were identical; maybe they had started out as one and been split or maybe they were identical but one was male and one was female. We did not have the split part figured out yet, but if we philosophized enough we would figure it out. In any event, the important point was that twin souls were of identical souls; sometimes they were both on earth at the same time and sometimes one was already in heaven while the other was earth bound.

"That is really amazing, Mom." I thought it extraordinary that she felt she had met her twin soul. But then she dropped the heavy news.

"Lisa, when he turned so I could see face, he...he...he was turning...he was reaching back for me. He reached out a beautiful, perfect hand for mine...I mean for me to put my hand in his and continue upward."

I shuddered. "What happened next, Mom?"

"I don't know...I either woke or I don't remember. What I do remember is that I could hear the Hungarian instrument that sounds like an oboe. Whenever I hear the instrument it resonates in my spirit and brings sentiments for Hungary. When I heard it this time, it stirred my soul. Between the closeness I felt from him and the soul-stirring music, it felt real. I mean, I still feel it. It doesn't feel like a dream; it feels as real as if it truly happened."

She seemed shaken. "What did it mean?" we both asked each other and ourselves. One need not possess a doctorate in psychology or a sworn belief in parapsychology to see the symbolism of an angel coming to beckon her home. So now we were both shaken. But the obvious symbolism was perplexing....truly counterintuitive. My mother was only 48 years old! And she did not look or act a day over 29! She was brilliantly vibrant! She was incredibly alive! She radiated energy...a LOT of positive energy. She was one of those good people here on earth, who needed to be here on earth to spread her goodness to all those who needed it. It was utterly illogical to think the heavenly figure might have come to call for her passage from this world to the next. No! NEVER! It was impossible to fathom the appearance as a beckoning from another world.

A couple of weeks after Nonna told me that grandpa was coming to her, I sat at the edge of her hospital bed holding her hand while the cardiac surgeon told her there was no longer an option for surgery...that she could only expect to live for about two more years. The image of the lovelorn young man in the old postcard and the coincidental concurrent apparitions to Nonna of the same man–the love of her life—flashed through my mind. I sat on the edge of Nonna's hospital bed with confused thoughts tumbling through my mind. An other-worldly reuniting with the love of his life would be a marvelously joyful gain for Grandpa Nonno. But his good fortune would come at an overwhelmingly painful loss to me. The latter brought my thoughts to a numbing halt. I turned toward Nonna, forced a bleak smile on my face and begged God to help me think of the right words to say to soften the devastating blow of the surgeon's death sentence.

In my lifetime I will never have verification of what the dreams or apparitions were, or if they truly occurred. Whether they were true does not concern me. The apparitions lead me to the reassuring thought that there was a being with an incredible bond of love, reaching across universes to bring Nonna and mom to a place where they both could be enveloped in pure love. And these love-bearing beings have brought them to a place where I know they are at peace and one with a power of love so strong it is incomprehensible to us humans. What better could I want for Nonna and Mom, both of whom I dearly love? While I may not know the result of the apparitions for Nonna and Mom, my knowledge of the dreams and apparitions have brought deep peace and assurance to my grieving process.

It takes courage:

- Recognize that grief resolution may come through dreams.
- Consider that apparitions may be true.
- Accept there may be a healing and loving message for you in apparitions.
- Believe a loved one continues to envelope you in a bond of love after departing this world.

Chapter 4
Improving End-of-Life Care

What is our responsibility to loved ones and members of society as age or disability lead them to the closing stages of their lives?

On June 4, 1990, Jack Kevorkian brought a 54-year-old woman into the back of his beat-up old Volkswagen van. Unfamiliar with live human patients, Kevorkian jabbed the woman five times with a needle before he was successful at inserting an intravenous line into her arm. With bloodied hands and pants, he instructed the alert woman to flip a switch and release the lethal chemicals that would stop her heart. Although the woman had come from the state of Oregon, the incident took place in Oakland County, thus thrusting Michigan into the national spotlight in a debate about dying. Within hours after she died Kevorkian gave a series of media interviews where he claimed he used his suicide contraption "to force the medical and legal establishment to consider his ideas." In days following the woman's death media reports revealed that the woman was not terminally ill; rather she only recently had been diagnosed with Alzheimer's disease. Her sons did not approve of her assisted suicide; one son having played tennis with his mother shortly before she left for her death trip. A June 7, 1999, *New York Times* article reported:

> Many medical experts said yesterday that it seemed precipitous for an Oregon woman to commit suicide at the age of 54 after being told that she suffered from Alzheimer's disease. They explained that it is difficult to make a definitive diagnosis of Alzheimer's and that even after a diagnosis the patient's condition usually worsens only gradually...They noted that symptoms of the woman, Janet Elaine Adkins of Portland, were still mild enough that she was able to beat her son at tennis and carry on normal conversations...
>
> "Given the uncertainty about diagnosis, for a relatively young woman to do this is just a terrible waste," said Dr. Zaven S. Khachaturian, associate director at the National Institute on Aging in Bethesda, Md."
>
> ..."It's of utmost importance to take a careful medical history," said Dr. Steven H. Ferris, head of the Aging and Dementia Research Center at New York University Medical Center. "A lot of these other causes of dementia are treatable."

The headline news increasingly brought stories of deaths assisted by Kevorkian. The details revealed that the victims were not the terminally ill, suffering patients the public assumed. Of the more than one hundred people Jack Kevorkian assisted to their death, the vast majority did not have terminal illnesses and did not have a physician-patient relationship with Kevorkian. Neither did Kevorkian have a relationship with the victims' treating physician. Several of those assisted to death had *no illness whatsoever*. That fact unsettled my soul, the next fact pricking the unsettled feeling into alarm: several of the now dead people had a known and long history of depression or a mental health issue.

A compilation of the reported biographical statistics showed that the common characteristics of Kevorkian victims were: 1) non-terminally ill, 2) vulnerable, 3) women, 4) with depression. It weighed on me heavily–the facts continue to heavily weigh on me–susceptible women, non-terminally ill, depressed, several abused by the very husbands who brought them to Kevorkian for death, some whose husbands received life insurance payouts after bringing them to Kevorkian, were lost in a vigorous rhetorical debate about a "right to choose" to "die with dignity." To this day I solemnly view the dead as victims of a malevolent campaign.

The 1990s assisted suicide campaign thrust on the public reminded me of the late 1930s early 1940s propaganda campaign told to me by my Hungarian grandfather (*Nagypapa*) and Hungarian grandmother (*Nagymama*). My *Nagypapa* was well-educated, highly intelligent, and fluently spoke six languages. Both he and *Nagymama* spoke German, French, and English in addition to their native Hungarian language. I grew up listening to my *Nagypapa's* stories about fleeing from their ample country estate in 1945 as the Nazi's closed in from the West and the so-called Soviet "liberators" from the East. *Nagypapa* had a tall, proud stature yet a gentle soul. How would he tell his precious "Lilleke," as he affectionately called me, of the atrocities, torture, and killings he witnessed as he attempted to safely move his wife and two little girls across an insane European continent?

"Lilleke..." he would softly begin as I nestled next to him on the couch, my round, pixie haircut-framed face admiringly looking up at him.

"Lilleke. It is unconscionable the atrocities...the heartless torture and pointless cruelty…man has brought upon fellow man. But World War II was not the first time and it will not be the last time. History repeats itself, Lilleke. Remember that."

When I was in my early twenties I asked my *Nagymama* how it was that Hitler could ever have been elected by his countrymen. I will never forget the impact of her response on my young adult mind. It was one of those rights of passage from the naiveté of youth to the harshness of reality. Mine had been a revisionist's history. In the 1980s every person on the globe recognized Hitler was evil. But *Nagymama* described 1930s Europe as a time of recovering economy and relative calm after the turmoil and devastation of World War I. Her lifestyle in the Hungary of mid-to-late 1930s was of modest wealth and peaceful estate living. Soirees swirled with aperitifs served on silver heirloom trays by gloved servants. Rich pastries and decadent tortes were daintily consumed using engraved silver dessert forks; *kave eszpresszo* stirred noiselessly in petite demitasse cups. The gatherings were a vision of affluence and polite, proper etiquette. Despite the inhibited polite air, *Nagymama* explained that some of the well-educated, elite acquaintances engaged in intellectual political discussions. But many people in Germany were not experiencing comfortable, peaceful lifestyles. In fact, the economy and tension among European countries was strained. A young and visionary German named Adolf Hitler began touting his plans to rehabilitate and create a strong Germany.

Nagymama described how she heard well-educated, elite acquaintances talk of support for the German politician's general plans to create an economically solid Germany. *"What…educated people could actually have agreed with Hitler? It makes no sense…"* *Nagymama's* account had blown my twenty-year-old's view of reality. Knowing the sheer evil Hitler spit at the world, causing the deaths of innocent millions and the destruction of the exquisite and historic gems of Europe, by no means could I fathom any person who would have not recognized and rejected his malevolence.

I was sitting on the tapestry-covered couch in *Nagymama's* Malibu Canyon, California home. It was fifty years since *Nagymama's* high society parties in Hungary. I leaned forward, mouth agape with question. No word escaped. For a moment I simply beheld the sight before me. *Nagymama* was sitting in a velour-cushioned, short cane-backed chair, relaxed but even so, perfectly poised. I admired her in that moment. Although in her seventies, she held perfect posture, not a hint of widow's peak—even though at almost six feet of height she had a foot more height than most women. Her head tilted slightly back with the air of aristocracy with which she was born—even though Hitler's venom had stolen her official royal title. With steel-blue eyes and elegant, high cheek bones, her beautifully chiseled face looked more of Germanic origin than Magyar Hungarian.

"*Nagymama*! I don't understand! How could people not see how maniacal Hitler was? Tell me..."

Emphatically, with heavy accent of Hungarian language, *Nagymama* tried to explain:

"In the beginning, many people liked what they heard him say...that he was for a superior Germany. It wasn't that people were stupid. When he said 'superior' Germany, people thought he was mentioning a strong and secure country... prosperity for all of its citizens. Hitler was very enthusiastic during his speeches. Of course...to hear about living in a safe and prosperous country sounded good to many. People were persuaded. It was only after...several years after...the terrible, inhumane details and realities behind his plans... his true idea of a superior society was exposed."

I tried to imagine what benign generalities Hitler could have used to artfully co-opt ordinary citizens into such a ghastly plan. I sincerely tried. I even tried to imagine living in the 1930s, having survived World War I, living through the optimistic rebuilding of Europe, starting again to struggle as a society, listening to the politicians of the day. But I could never quite bring myself to sympathize with those who had believed in the up and coming Hitler. *Your lack of understanding is probably due to your knowledge of how devious his plans…how evil his deeds.*

It was around the time the 1990s assisted suicide rhetoric began emerging that my conscious mind was awakened to the fact that the extermination of thousands of Jews under the Nazi regime was actually based on the extermination model the Nazi's had developed *on persons with disabilities!* In October 1939, Adolf Hitler actually drafted a law authorizing the consensual and non-consensual euthanization of "life unworthy of life" or *Lebensunwerten Lebens*. Hitler's Nazi Euthanasia program, Aktion 4, was his health policy aimed to cleanse the German people of diseases and disabilities; his stated goal to eliminate "the useless eaters" or *Unnutze Esser*. The implementers of his policy set up six killing centers where the gas chamber concept was tested. Horrific! The gas chamber method of killing was perfected on persons with disabilities and used as training for the genocide of the Jewish population. Physicians and midwives were required to report to Aktion 4 authorities when it appeared newborns, children or adults had mental or physical abnormalities, including syphilitic diseases.

I remember the chills felt creeping up my spine and through my soul as I realized that recent social "health policy" also talked of "life unworthy of life" under the guise of "life without quality of life." In the latter half of the twentieth century and the beginning of the twenty-first we globally abhorred the demented terror perpetuated by the Nazis, yet by all appearances we were mirroring the Nazi Euthanasia Campaign today.

My mind flashed back to the image of regal *Nagymama*, patiently trying to help me understand how a sympathetically packaged program could have death and destruction at its core. *Was this current compassionate death campaign the same situation, a half century later?*

I ask you to compare two statements, one from Hitler and one from Kevorkian. The first, Hitler's health policy where the acknowledged public good was to cleanse the German people of disease and handicap in order to preserve the welfare of his national community (*Volksgemeinschaft*). The same national health policy was phrased as merciful to the person who was diseased or disabled. Pay close attention to the actual language of the euthanasia order, aimed to protect the public welfare, written on Hitler's personal stationary and signed by him:

> ...the authority of certain physicians... that persons who... are incurable can, upon a most careful diagnosis of their condition of sickness, be accorded a mercy death. (October 1939, translated from German)

Compare Hitler's order to the health policy of Kevorkian, who refers to himself as a mercy killer:

> ...the voluntary self-elimination of individual and mortally diseased or crippled lives taken collectively can only enhance the preservation of public health and welfare. (Court statement written by Kevorkian in August 1990)

When Hitler announced his public health plan, the headline on the front page of *The New York Times* read "Nazis Plan to Kill Incurables to End Pain." The news accounts sixty years later when the assisted suicide proponents announced *their* plan to "end the unbearable pain of the terminally ill" is the same...merely substitute the current assisted suicide proponents' names with the word "Nazis" in the title of the 1933 *New York Times* account.

It occurred to me that if the public could be persuaded in the 1930s and 1940s that it was good and merciful to exterminate people solely because they had a physical deformity or disability, the public sixty years hence could also be subtly convinced that terminating the life of someone with a disability was benign and benevolent. But sixty years later, with the same attempts at public seduction, I was, as a person identified as having significant disabilities, a target of masked compassion. In both instances the false compassion led to an increased devaluation of the lives of people who had illness or disability. With devaluation of the lives of people with disabilities comes desensitization of the right of those human beings to participate in society in the similar manner as non-diseased persons.

Desensitization worked well in the Nazi era and was working well in the 1990s as people began to believe disabled people in Michigan should seek death through Kevorkian. But the desensitization of people in Germany quickly slipped into belief that it was equally good to exterminate any population their leaders said were of less worth. Jewish neighbors were taken away in plain sight of non-Jewish, life-long neighbors, never to be seen again. Several of the notorious concentration camps were in close proximity to inhabited villages–close enough for the non-Jewish, non-disabled inhabitants to know exactly what was going on. Maybe there was passivity because of fear. Or maybe there was passivity because at some level they believed the message they heard–to end the life was an altruistic and beneficial act.

As the deadly compassion rhetoric began to rise in the 1990s, I reluctantly realized I needed to speak up–for thousands of vulnerable people with disabilities, if not solely for myself. I do not have a fear of public speaking and do not mind presenting or performing in public. I had made public presentations, singing performances, and public competition from a young age. In addition, my mother had formed the first guitar folk Mass in our parish after Vatican II loosened the Catholic Mass protocol in the 1970s. The St. Gertrude Parish Council and priest allowed her guitar group to perform at the newly sanctioned Saturday night Mass, the option least offensive to the traditional Catholics already offended at the thought of bringing a guitar into the church. As an eleven and twelve year old my mother had me sing and play percussion instruments with her five-member "Dawn's Light" music group. There I stood to left of the altar every Saturday evening Mass, singing in front of the congregation and bangin' that tambourine off my hip...*Amen sister*! To this day I am not inhibited to belt out a song in front of people. Give me a legal doctrine and I can talk for hours in front of 10 people—or 1,010 people—no problem. I can spit out three hours of non-stop speaking without apparent effort on the history of the text of the Constitution and how it has been manipulated into a "right to privacy" where the word privacy never appeared. But if the subject involves me disclosing any aspect of my personal life, I dread, thoroughly dread, the task of revealing it to an audience small or large. I am a very private person. The thought that I should speak out on the perils of assisted suicide meant I would have to talk about my disabilities in public. It meant that I would have to reveal my innermost beliefs, fears, and feelings as they related to being regarded as having a disability. At one point I decided the most comfortable and "safe" choice for my legal career was not to become personally involved. But then I heard in the back of my mind Nagypapa's gentle warning:

"...the heartless torture and pointless cruelty...man has brought upon fellow man...History repeats itself, Lilleke. Remember that."

I struggled between my conscience and my comfort zone. At the time I worked as policy staff for the Michigan Senate. During the period of internal struggle I attended one of the endless receptions held by interest groups who invite legislators and their staff for an opportunity to emphasize face-to-face the organization's position. I was standing adjacent to the table of typical mini-drumstick or counterfeit meatball-filled chafing dishes. A person in position to influence state law and policy was making polite talk about the more controversial bills currently before the Michigan legislature. At least three people joined in the conversation while attempting to nibble, balance appetizer plates, and drink from glasses with only two hands. The topic turned to the divergent assisted-suicide bills before the legislature. The lawmaker knew I had rheumatoid arthritis or had noticed the deformities in my hands as I struggled with my plate and glass. This person of influence unabashedly asked me: "I assume you are for assisted suicide...I mean...why would you want to live with all your problems and pain?" In the moment of stunned shock, I recalled the "life unworthy of life" or *Lebensunwerten Lebens* and the assumptions of the educated and influential people of the 1930s regarding what constituted life worthy of living. What about the fact I possessed a law degree and worked for some of the most influential people in the state of Michigan? What about the fact that it was 7 p.m. and I had already worked twelve hours analyzing research and providing guidance to legislators on the senate floor during session that day? That moment was the kick in the pants needed to "get over" my reluctance to share personal aspects I held closely private. I would speak out in opposition.

And so the public speaking tour began. It was not as if I had to search for opportunities to speak. I was an attorney who knew the laws. I was a person with not one, but two serious disabilities. I had spent time in a nursing home after my mother and grandmother had been killed in a car accident. At the height of my dependence on others I had been treated with dignity and affirmed as an important person. At the height of dependence I also had felt devalued and without support. Credentials and experiences...all in one person! My story: compelling and credible. Soon I was being asked to present at forums, debate on panels, or appear as the featured speaker. I presented in all media formats: in person, over radio, on television, and via the rapidly evolving Internet.

Appearing on a panel of experts in 1995 I was quoted in the *Bay City Times*:

> "I suffer from rheumatoid arthritis,
> as did one of the first four people that Dr.

> Kevorkian assisted to die…This condition, although painful, is not life-threatening and it concerns me to know that a doctor judged the quality of her life and decided that woman should not live."

On Sunday, April 7, 1996, *The New York Times* ran a headline in its Metro section:

The Right to Suicide, Some Worry,
Could Evolve Into a Duty to Die

I was quoted in the article, explaining from the perspective of a person with a disability:

> "People who are sick already feel that they are a financial and emotional burden to their families and to society…Now society is telling them, 'You have an option. You have the right to die.' For them, this translates easily into an obligation to die."

The New York Times article was evidence the issue of assisted suicide had reached a level of national debate. The U.S. Catholic Conference of Bishops sought a venue to accurately clarify facts about key issues in the assisted suicide debate. This national affiliation of Catholic Bishops organized a symposium to take place at the Columbus School of Law at the Catholic University of America in Washington D.C. The conference, scheduled for March 7 – 8, 1997 would be titled: *Life at Risk: A Closer Look at Assisted Suicide.*

In January 1997 I received a call from a U.S. Catholic Conference of Bishops representative:

"Would you give the perspective of a woman with a disability at the *Life at Risk conference*?"

Anxiety and disappointment rushed in with the question: *Oh no! I am scheduled for a total knee replacement less than a month before the presentation…but I have an important story to tell! Oh, Lord…how am I going to do this? Lord, show me a way!*

I was informed that I would be asked to tell my story during a conference session titled: *Voices of Experience*: Disability. Other confirmed presenters were heavy-hitter international and United States experts: Dr. Zbiniew Zylicz, Rozenheuvel Hospice, and Henk Jochemsen, Lindeboom Institute Center for Medical Ethics, both from the Netherlands, relating the inhumane realities of the quasi-legal Dutch euthanasia; Dr. John Keown, Cambridge University, London, discussing lessons from Britain, Canada, and Australian encounters with assisted suicide; Dr. Ira Byock, American Academy of Hospice and Palliative Medicine, providing humane and available alternatives to assisted suicide; Dr. Edmund Pellegrino, Georgetown University, contemplating medical ethics and the question of what is the patient's best interests; and Professor Cathleen Kaveny, University of Notre Dame Law School, presenting how economic pressures may effect assisted suicide for the poor and those with managed care health insurance.

C'mon. This is a remarkable opportunity for you to learn from the world's experts! It's an important opportunity to offer your perspective. You've got to figure out a way to attend! Think. Think! This is your third knee replacement. It's been about eight years but you recall enough to know that you will be in a full leg brace about two weeks after the surgery. You can figure out a way to get to the airport and to a Washington, D.C., hotel in a leg brace. You've done it before. C'mon. Just say yes! Then pray about it and it will all work out…

I accepted the offer to present at the *Life at Risk* conference and explained that I would be in a full leg brace and would need wheelchair accommodations.

The surgery date arrived to remove the old artificial knee and replace it with another artificial knee. So too, arrived surgical complications. The knee prosthesis that had been implanted in my bone during the first total knee replacement in 1987 had become defunct. Simply put, the plastic parts of an artificial knee resemble the thick layer of cartilage that coats the ends of the upper leg bone (femur) and lower leg bone (tibia) that meet to form a normal knee joint. The cartilage, and in my case the plastic slides smoothly against each other, enabling the knee to bend easily while walking or climbing stairs. Unknown to me or my surgeon was the fact that I had walked too long on the artificial knee. Not only had I worn through all the thick plastic discs, I had ground the metal end of the upper leg against the metal end of the lower leg. Step after step, I ground fine metal shavings into the knee joint. Each time I bent my knees to sit or stand the metal dust forced deeper into surrounding bone and tissue. It was a hidden evil: the surrounding muscle and bone tissue did not like the foreign grated metal, creating a mess of metal, inflamed tissue, and irritated bone deep within my knee joint. A high pain tolerance allowed me to keep walking on the infested, inflamed knee long past what normal people would have tolerated.

During the surgery I had a local epidural and had been conscious enough to hear the surgeon remark, "Oh, no!" A dismayed utterance of "Oh, no!" is never a good sign during surgery. The evil infestation had been exposed! The surgeon had cut through muscle tissue to reveal the metal parts of the prosthesis but was shocked to discover a lot of metal shavings mixed in with disintegrating muscle tissue.

The surgeon stepped around the surgical screen that separated us to show me a small Styrofoam cup of the putrid mixture. In my sedated state it looked like pencil shavings loosely stirred into ground turkey. The integrity of the femur and tibia bones was compromised due to months of my body's angry immune reaction. The situation jeopardized the ability for the stem of the new artificial knee to fit snugly into the shaft of the femur and tibia and to have healthy bone grow around the metal stems.

I heard the surgeon address me from the opposite side of the surgical screen:

"I need to be forthright with you. I am not sure we will be able to find a prosthesis with a stem large enough in diameter to fill up the space eaten away by the inflammatory process." *Oh boy...this does not sound good.*

"Do I have your permission to proceed as I find necessary, even if it means having to remove your leg from the knee down?"

I decided that in my present condition–lying naked and helpless, partially sedated, body part split open to the bone–it was better to not ask any additional questions.

"Yes, you have my permission to take any approach necessary...and doctor, thank you for trying your best."

"Okay then...let me get started. The surgery will last longer than the dose of anesthetic we gave you in your epidural. Therefore you are going to be put under general anesthesia."

The anesthesiologist was standing adjacent to my head. "Can you wait a few seconds before putting me under? I want to say a prayer." *Lord! I need you! I need you to come here! Stand at my side and place your hand strongly on my shoulder. I need your help to protect me and to give wisdom to the doctors and nurses. Angels! Fly into this room! Float above the surgeons and nurses. Steady them! Guide them!*

"Okay. Thank you. I am ready." Instantly my world turned dark; dark as the deepest, drug-induced knock-out can take you.

I woke to the mind-blowing shock of extreme post-surgical pain. I tried to reach out and feel for my leg. *Is my leg attached? Do I have a full-leg cast?* Later, I learned the surgeon had to cut away too much damaged bone to use the standard prosthesis, but he was able to insert an older, larger model prosthesis he had developed years ago. It was a miracle that he worked a solution so I would actually be able to walk! It was a miracle that somewhere in the bowels of the University of Michigan Medical Center one outdated, abandoned prosthesis sat on a shelf, was located, and was successfully implanted into my femur and tibia bones. *Thank you Lord for the miracle! Oh thank you!* To ensure the miracle was the kind that endured, the surgeon placed me in a full-leg plaster cast–it weighed tons! *What about your plan to travel with a lighter-weight leg brace?*

Thursday, March 6, 1997, arrived quickly. Too quickly.

Despite bitter, icy conditions in Lansing Michigan, my weighty, bungling cast and I made it into the first row—in those days the handicapped or infant row—of the Northwest Airline plane.

There is extra leg room in this row. You can keep your leg elevated if you hook the plaster heel into the magazine pouch on the wall ahead of you. The flight is less than three hours. You can do it. The only time you will have to keep it at a lowered level is upon take-off and landing. You can do it!

But the metal shavings challenge of a few weeks prior was not the only surprise of the month. Forty-five minutes went by and the plane did not push back for takeoff. The captain came over the public speakers to announce that ice had accumulated on the wings of the plane and they were waiting for the de-icing crew to arrive. Another half an hour went by. My leg ached and throbbed with each pulse. It felt as if it were swelling—desperately struggling against the restriction of the cast for freedom and relief. I could feel the pressure fighting to burst out of the restrictive, thick plaster restraint. I had to fight feelings of claustrophobia and the desire to find a hammer and smash the cast for liberating relief.

Because the doors had been secured and cleared for take-off, no one was allowed to get out of their seat. It was no longer simple to keep my leg elevated. Pains shot through my leg, radiating from my spine to my toes. I could not shift my weight more than ever so slightly. Doubts and fear were ping-ponging through my mind and chest. *What are you doing here? What were you thinking? It was a miracle the surgeon was able to rescue your ability to ever walk again on this leg! Why would you risk that by thinking you could fly by yourself on a plane in the middle of winter? You are going to begin a new job as staff to the Michigan Senate in just eleven days!!! Why would you ever risk that phenomenal opportunity? You promised the Senate Majority Counsel and Senate Majority Leader you would start on March 17th. You are risking your ability to walk, your future career and your commitments!*

I called myself all kinds of names and laid on every type of blame. I tried not to think that I might have to go to the bathroom because there was no way for me to get to the bathroom until I was deplaned. As my anxiety grew, so did my imagination. *You are a prime post-surgical candidate for a blood clot. You cannot even take precautionary measure to move your legs or increase blood circulation in your legs!* What the Northwest pilot and flight crew failed to inform us was that Northwest Airline union employees, including repair crews and de-icing crews, were on a slow-down strike. A skeleton crew provided services at a deliberately delayed pace. It was hours before we departed. It was with God's grace and a lot of courage that I survived the flight and managed the next several days' endeavor around Washington D.C., sitting hours long in an auditorium and navigating a hotel and airports. And with that same determination, born of duty and fueled by courage, I delivered my story on that Friday afternoon, 7th of March 1997, merely two weeks after undergoing a treacherous major surgery. The story pointed out that as society devalues its citizens with disabilities, it seduces justification for ending those lives—including euthanasia and assisted suicide.

In the decade-long debate concerning physician assisted suicide, there has been a great quantity of written and spoken rhetoric on achieving a "dignified death." Most of it is untrue or unrealistic. The lines go something like this, "Each individual should have the right to end her life in a dignified manner without having to live in diapers or pain or dependent on others."

The most honest piece I have ever read on death with dignity came from U.S. Congressman and former Michigan Senator John "Joe" Schwarz. At the time he wrote about death with dignity Senator Schwarz was the President Pro Tempore of the Michigan Senate. In that role he had a reputation for being outspoken, stubborn, and sometimes ill-tempered. He also has a compassion for others that runs chasms deep. By trade he is a surgeon, maintaining his practice on the days he was not presiding over the Senate. In his three decades of practicing medicine, he had witnessed many people die: from horrible deaths in the jungles of Vietnam to domestic deaths as a result of highway accidents or lingering deaths from chronic debilitating diseases. The most painful for him was the death of his beloved wife from cancer.

The week after the U.S. Supreme Court rendered its 1997 decisions in *Washington v. Glucksberg* and *Vacco v. Quill* proclaiming there was no right to assisted suicide, Senator-Doctor Schwarz sat at his kitchen table, the same table at which he had sat thousands of times before with his wife, and wrote a piece for *The Detroit News*. The essay is entitled "No Escaping the Indignity of Death." It is not possible for me to paraphrase his work and recapture his honesty and eloquence, and I am grateful to him for allowing me to reprint a portion here.

> I believe, and will always believe until the day I'm the protagonist, that witnessing the death of a fellow human being is the most humbling and heart rending of all life's experiences.
>
> Nonetheless, people who are going to die should be allowed to die. No one gets out of the contract. As life starts to wane, we are given a certain awareness that time is almost up and we'll soon be moving on.
>
> The scenario begs the question: "What is death with dignity"?
>
> Death with dignity has become a catch phrase for those who want to write into statute those things we can and cannot do in the environment surrounding the end-of-life.
>
> The spinmeisters for legalizing assisted suicide would have us believe their position is simply a natural progression of the ways and means of dying. They are self-congratulatory in the deftness of their

> deceit. Death with dignity is an oxymoron, a contradictory phrase. Those who have seen death many times would validate that fact.
>
> Death is sudden and tragic, or lingering and expected. It is painful or quiescent. It visits both young and old. It is never pretty.
>
> People *live* with dignity; death itself is not dignified.
>
> Spare me from the contorted logic of "death with dignity". Allow the terminally ill to die with compassionate care. Allow the disabled to live without fear that they are "disposable."

By the early months of 1998, the phrase "choice in dying" had joined its sister buzz phrase "death with dignity" in saturating the media's rhetoric on assisted suicide. Several legislative bills had been introduced in the Michigan Legislature competing to either legalize assisted suicide or to deem assisted suicide a criminal act. Senate Bill 200 sought to criminalize the act of assisting in a suicide or attempted suicide. Senate Bill 200 had passed the Michigan Senate in December 1997. The competing senate bill to legalize assisted suicide had not passed the Senate. Because Michigan was a Bi-Cameral state, Senate Bill 200 needed passage in the House and signature by the Governor before becoming law. On its passage by the Senate, the bill was sent to the House and was taken up in the House Judiciary Committee. The buzz around the Capitol was that the House Judiciary Committee had sworn to kill SB 200 and instead vote out its version of an assisted suicide legalization bill.

In my role as Senate Judiciary Committee Counsel and Senate policy advisor I had staffed all the Senate Judiciary hearings on Senate Bill 200 and its competing bill. I was asked to follow the House Judiciary Committee hearings on SB 200 as much as possible.

The House Judiciary plan to pass a pro-assisted suicide bill must have reached the streets. Dozens of people with disabilities showed up, whether by wheelchair, carts, crutches, or feet. People with terminal illnesses, chronic illnesses, painful illnesses, debilitating illnesses, deforming illnesses, AIDS, multiple sclerosis, and paraplegia appeared and endured hours-long waiting to have an opportunity to speak. God bless them. As physically and logistically challenging as it was for some people with disabilities to reach the House Judiciary hearings, they did. And let me tell you that if you are a wheelchair user or need to use arm-brace crutches, it is not an easy feat to reach a House Committee room in the Michigan Capitol building.

The Michigan Capitol, dedicated in 1879, was a glorious domed building with four wings formed in the shape of a cross. But it was built before the automobile, and what now existed as the bottom floor was originally used to quarter the legislators' horses. There are dozens of granite steps leading to majestic but monstrous walnut entrance doors. Needless to say, it was not accessible to motorized wheelchairs or people with mobility issues. The Michigan Capitol Committee made a grand attempt at accessibility during the renovations of the early 1990s. There were a few accessible parking spaces, a barrier-free entrance, and an elevator at the north side of the building. The three House Judiciary Committee meetings were held in the House Committee rooms on the 3rd floor, north wing of the Capitol. For a person with mobility issues it was enough of a feat to reach the 3rd floor of the Capitol building. But when the elevator door opened, a standing crowd of lobbyists, legislators, and legislative staff blocked ingress and egress. Shoulder to shoulder expensive suits rubbed as each crammed person worked his interest. There were loud-talkers, fast-talkers, lean-in-close-to-share-a-secret-or-make-a-deal talkers. In combination the persuaders created a roar above which a wheelchair user could not be heard to ask, "Excuse me! May I get through please?" A six foot high wall, at least twenty feet deep in most instances, stood between the person with a mobility issue and the House Committee Room. It took a grand effort to part the crowd and to forge a path to the House Committee room. But those people with serious disabling conditions—chair users, crutches users, people limping, and people weak from illness—overcame physical obstacles and persevered until they arrived at the House Committee room to face their elected leaders and express their opinion at one of the three January 1998 hearings.

Even though the trek was a tremendous challenge, people with disabilities believed their lives were at risk. And they told their elected officials so. Almost every person with a disability who testified gave passionate testimony against allowing assisted suicide to be legalized. I sat through every Senate and House hearing regarding the assisted suicide bills of the 1997-1998 legislative session. With lined pad of paper and pen I kept a tally of the number of people who testified for and those who testified against assisted suicide. My unofficial tally and the committees clerks' official tally showed the same: overall the majority of people testifying were against assisted suicide. It was a startling statistic to many of the non-disabled, pro-assisted suicide bill sponsors and proponents. They believed that anyone with a disability would obviously want to end her life. Why struggle, right? How could life be worth living, right? The media had been reporting polls claiming that when asked if people wanted to spend their last days of life in pain, they would rather have the choice to end their life. Importantly, when pinned to disclose the exact questions asked while polling, it was revealed they were loaded heavily to procure an assisted suicide answer. Even more important was that the majority of people with disabilities was vehemently against assisted suicide, and impressed on the legislators and public the reality that assisted suicide devalued their lives and placed societal pressures on them to die.

The spin doctors of the pro-assisted suicide campaign tried an appeal of "Those white, Christian right-to-life fundamentalists are trying to take away your choice to die!" But in my observation, the most vocally opposed to assisted suicide were not healthy, right-to-life, religious. No, they were people with disabilities; rich and poor, religious and agnostic, Caucasian and non-Caucasian. In the assisted suicide cases before the U.S. Supreme Court in its October 1996-1997 term, Not Dead Yet, a national organization of people with severe disabilities, and American Disabled for Attendant Programs Today (ADAPT), a national organization of people with severe disabilities who had been institutionalized in nursing facilities, filed a Brief *Amici Curiae* in the case. I participated in a couple of the national teleconferences that took place as the Counsel of Record, Stephen Gold and the founder and president of Not Dead Yet, Diane Coleman, J.D., outlined and developed the Brief. May heaven bless Diane. She has significant disabilities and had used a motorized wheelchair since she was 11 years old. Yet nothing held her back from obtaining her law degree, sitting on boards of directors, being interviewed on nationally syndicated talk shows, and pretty much making all the healthy walking folks look like slugs. The "Interests of *Amici Curiae* for Not Dead Yet" stated that the organization:

> "...opposed the legalization of assisted suicide because it singles out people with significant health impairments for assistance to die, denying them the equal protection of laws and medical practice standards automatically applied to healthy individuals who are suicidal." *Brief of Amici Curiae, page 2.*

During the 1996 *amici curiae* planning conference calls the experiences of many people with severe disabilities in the two organizations were summarized to appear in the brief. Highlighted was the irony that a "right to die" was to be granted before accessible health care, adequate attention to depression, and appropriate in-home support services for living independently be made available. Also highlighted was the fact that there existed a societal devaluation of people with disabilities for which no adequate safeguard could exist within legal assisted suicide, especially in a climate where health care rationing was main stage in the national news and consequently,

> "untimely deaths are ultimately acceptable in the interest of the 'greater good'. *Brief of Amici Curiae, page 30.*

The first week of January 1997 I found a last minute flight from Lansing, Michigan and flew to Washington, D.C. Even though I knew it would be very limited, I wished to play a very minor part in the mock courtroom preparation of attorneys for oral argument in the *Vacco v. Quill* and *Washington v. Glucksberg* assisted suicide cases. State of Washington Attorney General Christine Gregoire had flown in to defend the State of Washington's anti-assisted suicide policy. Similarly, State of New York Attorney General Dennis Vacco had arrived to defend the State of New York's anti-assisted suicide policy. Most of the preparation had already occurred before I arrived. The morning of January 8, 1997, had a bitter chill. I can still feel the chill in my bones and the ache in my feet as I stood in line in front of the prestigious United States Supreme Court building for the chance to be seated and witness the arguments in front of the nine men and women of the highest court in the country. On the sidewalk in front of the U.S. Supreme Court building was a line of Not Dead Yet and ADAPT members, crouched in their wheelchairs against the biting January cold. Those able to grasp with mitten-covered hands held signs of protest. Others had signs fastened to their wheelchairs. "I'm Not Dead Yet!" and "I Want to Live!" were heroically displayed. I started to panic at the thought that my knees, ankles, and feet might not hold out the length of time I needed to wait for a seat, or the winter cold would settle in my bones. I only had to look behind me at the dedicated people with much more severe disabilities, much more susceptible to the bitter weather, who without complaint demonstrated for hours outside the building where lofty arguments that impacted their lives took place.

Not Dead Yet, ADAPT, and their U.S. Supreme Court *amici* briefs in effect say that "Choice in Dying" is a misnomer because a choice of the services needed to live independently are lacking, and therefore a choice to die is premature, discriminatory, or can never be justified.

The best lesson I ever learned about the lack of choice came from one of the three January 1998 Michigan House Judiciary Committee hearings. It was a year after the U.S. Supreme Court arguments and six months after the U.S. Supreme Court issued an unequivocal pronouncement against the existence of a "right to die" in the U.S. Constitution. Up to testify was Al Swain. Al had credentials–a Master's Degree and Honorary Doctorate from Olivet College. Associate Director at the Center for Independent Living, Al helped people with disabilities find employment and housing, increasing their independence. Al also happened to be blind since childhood. He used a motorized wheelchair due to multiple sclerosis' paraplegic devastation. Al was African-American. To look at Al, people who did not know better might think he had been dealt the absolute lowest deck of cards possible!

In the January 14, 1998 House Judiciary Committee meeting the Chairman made opening comments about his belief: the will of the majority of the people of Michigan was in favor of assisted suicide. At the next House Judiciary Committee meeting, January 20, 1998, Al Swain had arranged a wheelchair transport van to deliver him to the Michigan Capitol, and had someone help guide him through the wings, elevators, and throngs of lobbyists to take a spot in the committee room unoccupied by a chair. The Committee Chairman picked up one of the many cards that had been filled out indicating a desire to give public testimony and called out the name of "Al Swain" to approach the witness table. As Al moved his chair in the direction of the person guiding him to the witness table, I observed the confident faces of the committee members. Al began his presentation loudly and clearly. It plainly appeared that the committee members assumed he would support their choose-to-die efforts. Righteous appearance fell from their faces when Al started to speak against assisted suicide. Far from being an assumed down-trodden, Al is one of the most witty, good-humored persons I know. An invigorating speaker extraordinaire! Al's compelling testimony:

> People talk about this as an issue about freedom and personal choice. Well, it is, but in the climate that we live in today it's not about real choices. Okay, here's what the choice (of assisted suicide) is like for persons with disabilities and poor people and minorities. You're standing on this cliff, there's a thousand foot drop below you. Well, you could jump or turn around. Wait... there's a man-eating lion behind you! What kind of a choice is that?

The chairman of the House Judiciary Committee, a Michigan Representative from the Detroit area, was also an African-American. I thought perhaps the Chairman was having difficulty believing someone with a multiple-dose of severe disabilities—somebody like Al—could experience a satisfying quality of life. Or maybe he was lacking knowledge of the connection between the lack of assistance Al needed to live and work independently, and feelings of despair. I am not sure. From what I recall the conversation went something like this:

> Judiciary Chairman: "I want to note that it is very troubling for me that the handicapper associations seem to have a problem with assisted suicide...I don't see this as a handicap issue."
>
> Mr Swain: . . ."Let me ask you this. Did you ever have a bad toothache?"
> Judiciary Chairman: "Yes."

Mr. Swain: "A bad headache?"
Judiciary Chairman: "Yes."

Mr. Swain: "Do you make the best decisions under those circumstances? You want to do anything you can to get rid of the toothache or the headache, right? When you are having the toothache or headache you may say I will just blow my head off and make this toothache stop. Tomorrow when you are at dinner enjoying steak you will say, 'boy, I'm glad I didn't blow my head off because this is a really good steak.'"

In his opening remarks the Judiciary Chairman made a public statement about how he was representing all his constituents' needs, opinions, and beliefs as their elected official to the Michigan House of Representatives. He was also representing all of Michigan and its citizens' opinions as THE powerful Chairman of the House Judiciary Committee. So, Al set out to educate about the needs, opinions, and beliefs of Michigan citizens. He explained to all committee members that for people with disabilities whose only options are life in a nursing home or assisted suicide, there really is no "choice" because both options stink. Further, he added that not until more money or programs are available for independent living, should anyone even think about assisted suicide:

"Time would be better spent on legislation that would shift funding to more community-based living programs to give people some real choices."

Al followed the explanation with illustrations pointing out Michigan's current lack of options.

Have you ever thought about how a quadriplegic—whose ability to control muscle is limited solely to opening her eyes and moving her lips—can meet her most basic

> need if her unreliable personal-care assistant does not show up in the morning? Society does not set a rate of pay for personal care assistants sufficient enough to ensure an adequate number of decent people seek those care-taker jobs. Yet the quadriplegic is utterly vulnerable to the quality of a caretaker; whether and how she will be fed or bathed in the morning, whether her valuables and money will be stolen from her home.
>
> Or how a paraplegic, dependent on a wheelchair van service to bring him to work in the morning, can maintain employment if the unreliable, expensive transport service is late on some days and fails to show up on other days? It does not matter if the person with a disability is exceptionally responsible or excels in his work performance; if his transportation to work is unreliable his employer may be inclined to terminate his employment.

But the Chairman did not let up on Al. He continued to pursue the quality of life issue with Al. Al, respectful, but with humor in full force, gave a teaching I have never forgotten. He did not endorse the Chairman's suggestion that a physician should make the decision about when a person is a candidate for assisted suicide.

> If I would be described to a physician—blind, multiple sclerosis, paralyzed—the physician would have a very dismal picture to base a decision on. But, man...*I love my wife. I love my job. I travel all over and I love it...I'm having a damn good time!!!!*

The room resounded with laughter. Even the Chairman laughed. But Al's "no acceptable options = no real choices" point was made. Michigan citizens with disabilities had clearly won the education war for the day. I wondered if the Chairman began to fear losing the committee member votes he needed to win a majority vote on his assisted suicide legalization bill. He also needed those votes to kill the assisted suicide ban bill that had passed the previous month in the Senate and was now simultaneously in front of his committee. My suspicions of his fear were confirmed when he quickly adjourned the meeting until a later date.

The 1998 election cycle was one of the most extraordinary in the history of the state of Michigan. The same year that the assisted suicide proposal was on the ballot, Michigan citizens would vote for Governor of the State of Michigan. John Engler ran against Geoffrey Fieger, Jack Kevorkian's unscrupulous, outspoken lawyer. Geoffrey Fieger had won the August 1998 Democratic primary. John Engler had served two previous terms and with Michigan's economy thriving, was a popular incumbent. With a proposal on the ballot that would legalize assisted suicide in Michigan if a majority of citizens voted for it, the issues of end-of-life care, pain management, and assisted suicide frequently arose while campaigning. Governor Engler hit the issue head-on, exclaiming more needed to be done to improve end-of-life care, health care and pain management. With his Cabinet Member, James Haveman, Director of the Michigan Department of Community Health, a plan was put in place to create a consortium of organizations interested in improving end-of-life care. The consortium would work collaboratively to meet shared concerns and to form a single access point of end-of-life care resources: The Michigan Circle of Life. Director Haveman gathered critical groups in his conference room in the Lansing, Lewis Cass Building. Hospice of Michigan, health care organizations, physician groups, medical schools, and Ele's Place, a unique and desperately-needed organization for children grieving the loss of a parent, met to share knowledge and resources. The group focused on preserving the dignity and rights of people with a terminal or chronic illness. The Michigan Circle of Life priorities:

- Programs such as hospice that provide quality care for persons with terminal illness
- Programs for persons with chronic illnesses to reduce suicide ideation through better understanding and use of improved pain management
- Educational programs for health care professionals and faculty in managing pain, providing palliative care and suicide prevention
- Distribution of an interactive Easing Cancer Pain CD program
- Increasing awareness about existing tools to help make end-of-life decisions such as the Michigan Dignified Death Act, the Michigan Patient Bill of Rights, and the durable power of attorney for health care

While Governor Engler heralded the Michigan Circle of Life as an opportunity for critical stakeholder input as well as citizen educational tools, he promised, if reelected, he would focus on real changes to bring end-of-life improvements to the state of Michigan.

On November 4, 1998, a headline in the *Lansing State Journal* read, *Governor's Race Ends as Expected.* The article read:

> Republican Gov. John Engler won a landslide victory over Geoffrey Fieger Tuesday, burying the Democrat under the weight of his own words.

The November 4, 1998, the *Lansing State Journal*, other Michigan papers, and a *New York Times* op-ed also heralded the sound defeat of the assisted suicide ballot proposal by a resounding two-to-one margin. Within one week of the screaming defeat, the coalition of groups pushing appropriate compassionate care as an alternative to the assisted suicide ballot proposal–the Michigan State Medical Society, the Michigan Osteopathic Association, the Michigan Hospice

Association, the Michigan Association of Homes and Services for the Aging, the disability rights group Arc of Michigan, the Michigan Catholic Conference, the Michigan Right to Life, and the Michigan Family Forum–began running ads urging end-of-life options as an alternative to assisted suicide. The president of the firm that produced the television ad, Gary Pokorny, was quoted in the same article as saying,

"We should be thinking about killing the pain, not the patient."

Kevin Kelly, the managing director and lobbyist for the Michigan State Medical Society was quoted in the *Traverse City Record-Eagle* as saying the Medical Society's new theme was physician-assisted living:

> Many of us have read *Tuesdays with Morrie*, a book about the end-of-life by Mitch Albom. Tuesdays with Morrie gives the point of view that physician-assisted living can be wonderful...That scenario could take place every day for people in Michigan.

Laurie Orlando, president of the Michigan Hospice Association was quoted in the *Oakland Press* as saying the fight to educate people about the perils of assisted suicide,

...mobilized us to let others know that this (hospice) is an option and a better option.

Director Haveman disseminated facts about the Circle of Life program to many news outlets, emphasizing its mission–to empower people with information–thereby promoting rights and promoting dignity for people with terminal illnesses or with chronic illnesses. Director Haveman highlighted the unique aspect of the Circle of Life program: a single stop resource for end-of-life questions.

As I flipped through the daily clips of Michigan news stories, I was relieved–and thrilled–to see that many newspapers picked up and reported Director Haveman's vital information about end-of-life resources. There were articles in large city papers. *Great! Now many will see!* There were articles in small rural papers. *Fantastic! The word is spread to more isolated regions of the state!* I believed the articles were critically important because they delivered information about end-of-life services available to each Michigan citizen at that moment.

Within months of being sworn into office for an extraordinary third term, Governor Engler fulfilled his campaign promise of making additional, strident efforts at improving Michigan end-of-life care. Executive Order 1999-4, signed by Governor Engler on January 24, 1999, established the Michigan End of Life Care Commission. Shortly after issuance of Executive Order 1999-4 I had a second job interview with the Director and Deputy Director of the Policy Division within Governor Engler's Office. The position for which I was interviewing was Health and Human Services Policy Coordinator. The major issues I had been working on in the Senate, Lieutenant Governor Connie Binsfeld Children's Commission child welfare legislation, a welfare reform package, legislation to ban partial birth abortion, legislation to ban assisted suicide, legislation to ban cloning, all had been passed and signed into law or dissolved with the end of the 1998 legislative session. I was ready for the next career step.

Oh, Lord, please…I know I should be deferring to your Will…but to work for Governor Engler on health and human services policy would be an extraordinary opportunity to use the culmination of my life and career experiences and knowledge!!! I had a deep and abiding respect for the Senate Majority legislators. I believed in the laws they sought to amend or enact and worked diligently to assist them in their causes. But I also believed in the policies and positions of Governor Engler. What I had witnessed was a governor who did not take actions for show; he took actions toward progress, toward making Michigan a better, safer, healthy and economically-sound state. The profound respect only deepened as I worked for him.

On the very first day as staff to Governor Engler, I was

briefed on the priority policy projects attached to my new position. On the top of the list for the Governor: the Commission on End of Life Care. As such, a meeting with Director Haveman, the Governor's Special Projects Coordinator, and the Governor's appointments director was promptly scheduled. The first meeting's task was to develop a list of the types of experts needed to fulfill the full panoply of information critical for addressing all aspects of end-of-life care. Potential names of Michigan experts were to be compiled, from which the Governor was to appoint to the End of Life Care Commission.

Every governor's office has an appointments office. The function of the appointments office is to coordinate relevant individuals as potential appointees to various committees and commissions called for by statute or executive order. An age-old practice has been to appoint individuals who share political views similar to the governor. In fact, many Michigan statutes direct a governor to appoint members affiliated with either the Republican or Democrat parties. Not so with regard to the Commission on End of Life Care appointees–political affiliation was not to be a decisive factor. The Governor desired all opinions and the best able to provide those opinions–without regard to political affiliation.

The Executive Order, copied in part below, displays the breadth of end-of-life aspects to be addressed by the commission and affirms the Governor's commitment to include all input:

EXECUTIVE ORDER No. 1999 – 4
MICHIGAN COMMISSION ON END OF LIFE CARE
MICHIGAN DEPARTMENT OF COMMUNITY HEALTH

WHEREAS, the citizens of Michigan endorse humane and dignified treatment during life and at the end-of-life. Ninety percent of all citizens will experience a terminal phase of disease prior to death; and

WHEREAS, physician-assisted suicide raises moral and ethical questions for physicians, policymakers, patients and their families; and

WHEREAS, last November, Michigan voters were offered the choice of whether or not the state should decriminalize the practice of physician-assisted suicide and voted overwhelmingly to reject such a plan; and

WHEREAS, although many laws to address end-of-life issues exist and ensure individual autonomy in health care decisions, the individuals are often unaware of their right to make decisions to receive, continue, discontinue or refuse medical treatment; and

WHEREAS, research indicates that barriers exist to adequate and appropriate use of prescription drugs for pain management and for the provision of end-of-life care; and

WHEREAS, the quality of end-of-life care is dependent in part upon the quality of the education and training of present and future physicians, nurses, and other health care professionals…; and

WHEREAS, the public and many private organizations including, but not limited to, health professional organizations, religious organizations, and trade associations have established committees and working groups to study and recommend actions to improve the quality of end-of-life care. The opinions and recommendations of these organizations and the public are considered of great value…

NOW, THEREFORE, I, John Engler, Governor of the state of Michigan, pursuant to the powers vested in me by the Constitution of the state of Michigan of 1963 and the laws of the state of Michigan, do hereby order the following...

Charge to the Commission:

-The Commission shall recommend model state and institutional policies with respect to end-of-life care... including an examination and compilation of the best ideas of multiple groups currently engaged in examining end-of-life issues...

-The Commission shall identify and evaluate any existing barriers that result in inadequate end-of-life care in Michigan and, where appropriate, make recommendations for elimination or mitigation of such barriers.

-The Commission shall evaluate the adequacy of education associated with end-of-life care being provided in Michigan schools of medicine, Michigan schools of nursing and in other health professional education programs and, where appropriate, make recommendations to improve such education.

-The Commission shall survey availability and cost of public and private insurance coverage for hospice, pain management, and palliative care.

-The Commission shall inventory existing resources available to citizens for end-of-life planning and produce a guide of these resources for the general public.

So at the commencement of my new job, at the direction of Governor Engler himself, I set forth to interview and recommend individuals, from whom seventeen would be selected and appointed as members of the Commission on End-of-Life Care. After issuance of the June 1999 Executive Order, many interested organizations offered the name of a person it best felt could represent the expertise of its organization. Individuals nominated themselves. The appointment office files were reviewed for potential candidates. With a list of at least two dozen names, we began an interview process. With the mix of controversial health and human services hot-button issues my policy coordinator duties encompassed, it seemed nearly impossible to squeeze dozens of interviews into my already packed schedule. Each day a calendar was printed for me and placed on my desk. Almost every hour block of time was scheduled–sometimes scheduling meetings through the lunch hour! And the printed calendar did not account for unexpected but critical telephone calls from Executive Office staff, Cabinet members, or legislative liaisons.

I started working longer days–at least until 7 p.m. and on weekends if I wasn't at Nonna's in Detroit. If I was in Detroit for the weekend, a work-stuffed briefcase was my companion. I also had a problem...a problem I tried to hide. My arthritis-gnawed ankles and previously fractured feet bones were causing agonizing difficulty in walking. I was in the job of a lifetime–one for which I possessed immeasurable passion, one for which I never-minded how much time or energy needed to be expended–but my body was failing me. I did not want people to notice, but it was very obvious; I could barely manage the few steps from the private elevator to my office in the Governor's Policy Division.

I made an urgent plea to my Rheumatologist, Dr. Laing. Dr. Laing, in addition to unmatched intelligence, was an innovator.

> "Please...you've got to help me! I am fortunate enough to be working for the Governor...a man who is forwarding remarkable policies...but Dr. Laing...I can barely walk! The pain in my ankles and feet is so extreme it is nearly impossible to step

> down. Even when I am in bed at night…the stabbing at my joints jolts me awake with a cry for mercy! Please help me figure out what to do!"

I credit Dr. Laing with a great deal of my ability to achieve what I have accomplished in my life. His collaborative efforts in our doctor-patient team have kept me propped up and in forward motion. I was not exactly the easiest patient; my 110-pound body easily susceptible to the side-effects of my immuno-suppressive medication regimen. I typically fought against a suggestion to raise the milligrams of prednisone in order to manage flaring auto-immune diseases. And there was the other factor: I PUSHED my body to perform… probably stubbornly pushing past the healthy zone at times.

Dr. Laing laid out different immuno-suppressive medication configurations, until we landed on a medication regimen aimed at slightly more immuno-suppression, but not so much as to leave me unguarded for serious infection. No increase in daily milligrams of prednisone. *Oh. Thank heavens.* The number of Enbrel injections per week would also remain the same. But I would bump up the milligrams of methotrexate I took each week. *Not so great. Methotrexate causes quite a bit of cellular damage…hence its use as a chemotherapy agent at higher doses…but at this point I am most desperate to be able to function in my Governor's policy coordinator position…*

And so there I was: pumped with more immuno-suppression and walking with slightly more ease. The Governor's Special Projects Coordinator and I conducted commission member interviews in the small, unimpressive, third-floor conference room of the Romney Building Executive Office across from the Capitol building. I quickly felt ashamed for thinking I was busy. The candidates we interviewed were an extraordinary and invigorating cast of physicians, hospice directors, a legislator, nurses, two Executive Cabinet members, a lawyer and a minister. As if their credentials were not enough, the candidates threw heart and soul into their life's work. They were busy. They were phenomenal. And they drove in from all regions of Michigan for the interviews.

Each one of the commission members could herald an inspirational chapter, but I highlight three to give flavor to how extraordinary their lives and commitment to aiding others at the end-of-life:

Dr. Jeanne Lewandowski - There is one thing you remember about Dr. Lewandowski when you meet her… her gigantic, beaming smile. Before you even realize it you are utterly swept away by her incredible intelligence, vivacity and ability to achieve what she believes in. As a pediatric oncologist, she is often asked,

"Ummm…how can you care for dying kids? Isn't it depressing?"

Dr. Lewandowski's answers reflected anything but depressing. She tells of her belief that there is nothing more important than helping a kid leave this life in his own home, on his own couch, holding his own teddy bear, with his siblings playing around him, and his parent's lap to place his head during his last days. Dr. Lewandowski would do everything in her knowledge and power to assist that little child to be as pain-free, comfortable, and loved before cancer finally took that brief life.

I knew Dr. Lewandowski would knock the socks off the interviewers and make a fabulous contribution to the End-of-Life Commission. She did.

Sr. Mary Giovanni Monge - Dame Cicely Saunders is the person identified with founding the hospice movement. In 1960's England, Dame Saunders recognized that the need for directing care to a person in the process of dying was just as important as providing care for curative purposes. The medical model of health care in Britain was similar to that in the United States: focusing on curative treatment, awkward for attending to the physiological, psychological, and spiritual aspects of end-stage disease. Great change would have to manifest in the areas of medical education, attitude, and health care payment for the concept of hospice to occur. Dame Cicely Saunders took on the challenge and forged the foundation of what is known today as hospice.

In the early 1970s, knowledge of the phenomenal impact of hospice made its way to the United States. A group of compassionate health care professionals brought Dame Saunders from Britain to impart her wisdom and advice for starting hospice in the United States. One of those health care pioneers was Sr. Mary Giovanni Monge, a Catholic nun in the Felician Order, who possessed a bachelor's degree in nursing and a master's degree in nursing administration. Sr. Gio, as we refer to her, was determined to bring a hospice to the area of Livonia, Michigan. She faced many obstacles and setbacks. She did not give up. Instead, during those hindered years she studied about providing pain relief as end-of-life care. Pain relief in this situation is known in medical terms as "palliative care" as opposed to pain relief provided as part of a "curative" treatment regimen. She also studied alternative methods of pain relief and the multi-faceted needs of a person facing death. Her determination never dwindled.

About 11 years passed before Sr. Gio began attending to dying patients in their own homes in 1985. Sr. Gio recognized that there were situations where a person was not able to receive end-of-life care in his home. Sr. Gio began to pray and work toward a facility where she could administer hospice care. In 1993, Sr. Giovanni opened the first freestanding hospice center in Michigan. Her mother helped sew curtains for the patients' rooms. Her father contributed by fixing and maintaining the building. Today Angela Hospice has approximately 150 employees and serves more than 1,000 people a year. It has programs specializing in serving seriously ill children in their homes as well as for prenatal parents faced with knowledge their child may not be born alive. Although I seriously considered becoming a nun in my early twenties, if I ever do, I pray I will have the heart, spirit, and dedication of Sr. Giovanni. She is one of Michigan's most precious and illustrious gems, shining prisms of light onto many in what otherwise might have been their darkest hour.

I knew Sr. Gio's fervent diligence for Angela Hospice, and her commitments with the Felician Order absorbed more time than a day possesses. Yet I knew the Sr. Gio qualities that made Angela Hospice possible in the first place would be invaluable to the Commission on End of Life Care. She was appointed and–yes–her knowledge, zeal, and vision was invaluable.

James K. Haveman, Jr., - Director of the Michigan Department of Community Health. In 1999 the Michigan Department of Community Health had the second-largest budget in Michigan government with approximately 6,000 employees stationed in all areas of the state. I'm talking about administering health care services to nearly two million Michigan residents and managing a budget of $11 **billion**. It housed some of the most critical programs for Michigan citizens, including government-paid health care for adults and kids who could not afford their own health care, and mental health care for people who did not have the capacity to manage their own mental health care. Director Haveman was the person in charge of overseeing the budget, the employees and the programs of Michigan's top health authority. He could have used his position on the Commission on End of Life Care for status. He could have delegated the many long commission meetings and public hearings to his staff. He did not. Talking with me in the hallway of the Capitol building Director Haveman expressed his commitment:

> "End-of-life care is one of the most important issues we have. Whatever time I need to put in...whatever staff support may be needed to achieve the best results... that is what I will commit."

Director Haveman invested personal time and effort outside of what was required as a department director to the mission of improving the quality of end-of-life care.

Part of my role in Governor Engler's directive was as liaison between the commission and the Governor. I could hardly call it a "job." It was a privilege to be integrally involved in commission meetings and public hearings, fielding questions and concerns, reviewing commission recommendations, and coordinating policy changes needed to effectuate those recommendations.

The Michigan End of Life Care Commission traveled around the state of Michigan to gather public comment regarding the what, why, and how of improving end-of-life care. From the crowded Detroit-area metropolis to the sparsely populated Upper Peninsula: a total of 140 Michiganians attended the five public hearings; the majority providing testimony. It was obvious end-of-life care was as important an issue to the public, service organizations and health professionals, as to the members of the Commission and the Governor. All voices were heard. Notes were taken. Summaries were compiled. The summary of testimony from public hearings was sorted into categories:

Education-

-End-of-life care should be part of school curricula and continuing education for physicians, nurses, and other health care professionals. Education should address physical symptoms as well as psychological and spiritual needs.

-Education for the public and health professionals should include treatment options, hospice care, the right to refuse care, and organ donation.

Pain and symptom management-

-Physicians fear incurring sanctions when prescribing pain medications.

-The public needs to be made aware of the false perceptions about unwanted side effects, fear of addiction, and uncertainty about insurance consequences.

-Physicians who are specialists in palliative medicine should serve as resources for other physicians who are caring for patients at the end-of-life.

- Reimbursement for the transition from curative care to palliative care needs to be examined to determine if both types of care could overlap.

Reimbursement-

-The Medicare rule requiring hospice care be covered only when the physician's prognosis is that death is likely within six months leads to hospice referral only in the last days of life because physicians feel uncomfortable with making a prediction about when their patients will die.

-Medicaid does not generally provide for simultaneous curative care and hospice care, and as a consequence patients can be faced with an agonizing choice.

Public Awareness-

-There is a need to educate people about advance directives and the importance of having caring conversations with loved ones.

-The approach to end-of-life care varies with cultural beliefs, and end-of-life policy should address the unique issues of diverse populations.

The abundance of knowledge and recommendations culled from the public hearings enriched the Commission on End of Life Care findings. In addition, each member poured forth a wealth of understanding and counsel. The Commission was also remarkably fortunate to have nationally recognized end-of-life care experts give presentations or advice.

One such national figure was Dr. Ira Byock, the author of the book, *Dying Well, Peace and Possibility at the End of Life*, (Riverhead Press, 1997.) Dr. Byock and Dr. Jeanne Lewandowski both held leadership roles in the American Academy of Hospice and Palliative Medicine.

During one of the Commission meetings there was an illuminating discussion about the book *Dying Well*. Dr. Lewandowski emphatically described five phrases around which dying people desire to have caring conversations. They are:

I forgive you.
Please forgive me.
I love you.
Thank you.
Good-bye.

These five phrases were layered over what Commission members had previously outlined: there are fixed characteristics of a dying patient–age, gender, ethnicity, disease prognosis –but there are also variable aspects that can affect whether a patient experiences a "good death." Social relationships, caregiver availability, health insurance, and spiritual beliefs all play roles in the cognitive, psychological, and physical experience of dying. And all the varying aspects of dying interconnect. For example, as the Commission later pointed out in its report:

> A person who is depressed or experiencing a sense of existential meaninglessness may have a lower pain threshold, while patients who report spiritual fulfillment or good social support may be less bothered by their physical symptoms.
> *Report to the Governor/August 2001, page 35.*

Dr. Byock's five phrases provide the opportunity–a

platform–for the dying person to resolve past hurts with loved ones, an opportunity to thank them, to say "I love you!" and to say "goodbye". With the opportunity to express these fundamental elements of human connection comes peace of mind, peace of heart, peace of soul, and peace of spirit to die well and in harmony within oneself, with others and with the world. Any one of the five phrases can foster not only peace, but a sense of giving and being loved, a life review with others, and even humor, laughter and joy. These are vital elements to honoring a person's end-of-life.

With great effort on the part of some of the busiest people I know, the Commission members narrowed its findings to 46 policy recommendations. A few of the summarized, general recommendations were:

> The end of life is an important time in the life cycle of all Michigan citizens. People facing the end of their life should have optimal comfort and support.
>
> All Michigan citizens should be encouraged to engage in caring conversations with their loved ones concerning their expectations and wishes for end-of-life care, and to plan for their financial, emotional, legal, and spiritual needs at the end of life.
>
> A model of palliative care should be integrated into the various treatments, beginning at diagnosis of a life-limiting condition and continuing throughout the course of illness and beyond, regardless of treatment outcome.
>
> The lack of effective pain and symptom management is a public health issue that requires the highest level of professional and regulatory attention.

The Commission went on to give specific recommendations for removing barriers to and improving quality of care in the following categories: Professional education, pain and symptom management, reimbursement, long-term care, decision making for the end-of-life, and family issues. The Commission's report and recommendations were ground breaking and so significant to Governor Engler a press conference was scheduled. As the Governor's liaison, the press conference meant working with the Governor's scheduler to ensure key Commission members could attend. It entailed working with the Governor's communications staff on a simultaneous press release and to a very minor respect, a consult with his speech writer. Only an outline of a speech was needed for this event; Governor Engler had already absorbed the findings and recommendations, and with his commitment to improving care, he knew what he wanted to say.

On August 30, 2001, Rev. Thomason, Commission Chairman, Director Haveman, Director Wilbur, and I waited in the foyer area of the Governor's Communication Division. I had already been in the press auditorium – there was an exciting and fabulous turnout of press, already set with cameras, tape recorders, and note pads poised. The Governor's communications staff had distributed copies of the press release to members of the media. All members of the Commission who would attend were present and instructed when to join the Governor on stage. The Commission members jubilantly chatted in groups with the various interested parties also present for the press conference. The room was filled with an air of exhilaration. After a final exhausting push of effort to fine tune and complete the Commission report, the Commission could proudly and eagerly turn the report over to the Governor. *I can't believe this day has finally arrived! It is a pivotal day for every person in Michigan. Oh, thank you, God, that I can be here right now, that I am alive…that I can walk and that I can participate in this once-in-a-lifetime, monumental event!* Tomorrow I would start working with the Governor's legislative liaison to find senators and representatives to sponsor legislative fixes needed to implement the Commission's legislative recommendations. But for now, amid the elation and celebration, I needed to stay focused on the present task of staffing the governor for the press conference.

I had returned to the Communications Office and was explaining the press conference logistics to Rev. Thomason: where on stage to stand, who would follow the Governor's comments, media questions follow comments, and photo ops after conclusion of questions. I glanced frequently over his shoulder for my boss. *Yes! Everything is in order and we are right on time!* I saw the Governor exit the elevator from his office and head toward us. I left Rev. Thomason and quickly moved toward the Governor, so I could greet him in the hall, absent of guests. I walked with him and in as few seconds as possible told him everything was in order, and a marvelous turnout was assembled in the auditorium. I directed him toward the Commission Chairman for introductions.

Rev. Thomason, Director Haveman and Director Wilbur followed the Governor through the side entrance to the stage. I walked around to the public entrance of the press auditorium and stood against the wall as the Governor grabbed each side of the podium and started. His comments reflected those contained in the press release:

> When I appointed this Commission, I charged them with the responsibility of tackling an issue that is extremely complex, emotional and spiritual...This report reflects the very thoughtful and thorough approach taken by the Commission as Michigan seeks to lead the nation in providing support and quality care to those at the end of life.

His words spoke of the seriousness of the issues and gratitude to the Commission. His tone was of authentic concern, sincere appreciation and determination to effectuate the recommendations. Questions came from the press:

"Is the report available to the public?"

"How soon can the recommendations be implemented?"

"Do the recommendations require changes in law?"

"Is the Legislature expected to run bills without delay?"

Immediately after the Report was presented to the Governor, work began on drafting the Commission recommendations into legislative bills. Senators and House Representatives were approached as potential sponsors for the bills. There was typical political wrangling and budgetary concerns, but, remarkably, a package of fifteen end-of-life care bills were signed into public law by the Governor on the December 31, 2001, end of the Legislative session. That it took only four months for fifteen monumental bills to be passed by the Michigan House and Senate was an incredible testament to the recognition and desire for improvement in end-of-life care!

An official bill signing ceremony for the unprecedented package of bills was promptly arranged. My final duty as liaison to the Commission was to staff the Governor at the bill signing ceremony. The Commission on End of Life Care members and Senate and House sponsors gathered on the stage of the Governor's press auditorium. The podium present at the August 2001 press conference was replaced by a long desk on which unsigned copies of the fifteen bills ceremoniously awaited the Governor's pen. Photographers from the media and the legislature snapped photos as the Governor signed and held up bills. The last signature was my cue to ascend the steps and begin quickly arranging bodies for photo ops. Because members of the Commission and Legislature were already on stage I asked everyone to remain and flank to the left or right of where the Governor was seated. Photos were snapped. Bodies quickly rearranged–this time only the Governor and Commission members. More photo shots. Next, individual senators or representatives holding his or her respective bill next to the Governor had snapshots taken. The final photos taken were of directors of several interest groups who had afforded input and garnered support for the report and its legislation. I stood off to the side, herding the group that was to be next, requesting that they quickly enter and exit, and giving a suggested position to stand. Staffers were assigned to make sure key individuals had an opportunity for photo – not for their own photo opportunity. As a staffer, you do not expect a photo and rarely are you included in a press conference or bill signing related photo.

The last photo was snapped. A lone photographer relaxed from his animated photo-taking stance and started to twist his camera from the tripod. I walked from the shadow of side-stage and crossed mid-stage where Governor Engler stood talking with one of the Commission members, in order to exit.

"Wait!"

I heard Governor Engler's call, stopped and turned, seeking to determine whether he needed something.

"We need a photo with Lisa G…after all her hard work…"

The photographer remounted his camera while the Governor and I positioned ourselves. We each held up a corner of the signed House Bill 5260, the bill that would repeal the Official Prescription Program. The Governor whispered to me:

"This package is one of the most significant pieces of legislation I have signed. I know how much this also means to you. Thank you for all you did to make it happen."

"Governor, I know how much it means to you, too. Thank you for the opportunity to serve you and the people of the State of Michigan." My throat swelled with an overwhelming gratitude.

Whatever your politics may be, this was the John Engler I knew. This was the John Engler I loved. In the midst of all the pressing statewide issues he had already dealt with that day–and the critical items he urgently needed to get back to–he recalled how important improving end-of-life care was to me and wished to extend his gratitude for my effort. In one sense I was merely another paid staffer. Yet this was only one example of the remarkably thoughtful and generous Governor Engler–whether it was toward friend, co-worker and stranger–I witnessed over and over again.

A couple of months before his tenure ended, a large, brown envelope appeared on my office desk. I opened it to find an 8 ½ X 11 copy of the photo taken the day of the end-of-life care bills signing ceremony. Governor Engler had inscribed the photo at the bottom in thick, black pen:

To Lisa – You make me so proud.
You are so talented. Thank you for being so terrific!
With admiration,
John Engler

I sat there for several minutes, continuing to hold the photo in my hands. My eyes went to the photo and then to read the Governor's message, then back and forth again. At that moment, all the long hours, all the Commission debate, all the legislative wrangling, all of it, I knew, was worth it. The improvements in end-of-life care for Michigan as a result of the efforts of Governor Engler, his staff, and the Commission on End of Life Care have helped to ease pain, bring physical and emotional comfort, and bring pervasive peace to the dying and their loved ones. I remain proud and beaming with pride at how their efforts warmly touch the lives of people at one of the most significant–if not the most significant–moments in their life. In those precious moments I do not see the degenerating body or smell the non-obedient fluids or fear the impending morbidity. No. I see the opportunity–in those last, few, precious moments before death–to make them the most peace-filled and love-filled possible. I have thrown my heart and soul into many causes I believed important and noble. I consider the humble efforts toward improving the closing stages of a person's life –whether on a statewide level or on an individual basis–as one of the most important of my life's effort.

It takes courage:

- To have the caring conversation of "I forgive you. Please forgive me. I love you. Thank you. Good-bye."
- To spread the good news about the offerings of hospice: choice of home for final days, pain management, as well as psycho-social and spiritual support.
- To speak out for more supports for the aged and dying instead of being lulled to the neater, less-expensive, and more convenient propositions of health care rationing or assisted suicide.

Michigan Department of Community Health Director James K. Haveman with author in jet returning from Michigan Commission on End of Life Care public hearing, Marquette, Michigan, September 14, 2000.

Chapter 5

Honoring the End-Of-Life

My friend Kathy is an attorney who you could say is an expert in deciphering health insurance benefits. Kathy and I share a friendship that encompasses our deepest spiritual beliefs and a passion for advocating for kids with disabilities.

In a harsh series of unrelated events, Kathy experienced the unrelated cancer deaths of her sister, mother, and two brothers–essentially every living member of her immediate family—all within a relatively short period of time. Kathy had an involved relationship with her sister, mother, and brothers. It seemed that she had only buried one beloved family member when the next passed. One heavy grief was piled upon another. Despite the profound heartache, Kathy did all she could do to honor the end of each family member's life. Remarkably, Kathy put aside her own issues with grief and death to organize health care benefits and medical treatments, as well as provide hands-on, comforting care.

Kathy's only sister, Barb, was the first of the four to pass away. Barb lived toward the eastern side of the state of Michigan, just outside the city of Flint. Kathy lived as far west in the state of Michigan as is possible, with inlet waters of Lake Michigan lapping at her backyard. Barb, who lived alone at the time, was courageously waging a battle with lung cancer. More than a three-hour car drive separated them. Kathy invited her sister to live in her and her husband David's, home so she could join in the day-to-day battle against Barb's cancer. Kathy transformed the spare room on the main floor into Barb's room. It was there that Kathy cared for Barb after surgeries or during nauseating episodes of chemotherapy. It was also there that Kathy and Barb weighed the pros and cons of medical treatment options. This spare room was the war room for scouring health insurance policies, or for battling with various customer service representatives to receive authorization for treatment or durable medical equipment.

When it became apparent that her sister's care was going to move from curative treatment to palliative end-of-life care, Kathy sat on the edge of her sister's bed and asked,

"Sis...want to stay here a little longer?"

Kathy and David set forth to make Barb's transition comfortable and enveloped in love. Did they do so knowing that a person would be in the process of dying and would eventually die in their home? Yes. But they could see no more important role at that moment-for all of their lives -than to make Barb's passing as peaceful and loving as possible. Again, Kathy and David put aside their own issues with death and arranged for hospice to come into their home.

The back wall of Kathy and David's home is a series of floor-to-ceiling windows or sliding glass doors that face east onto a bayou. It is a majestic sight to watch the sunrise; the power of light conquering the dark, morphing into gorgeous fuchsia and peach pastels-staging a magnificent backdrop for the morning busyness of wildlife: humming birds flitting blissfully, ducks flapping merrily, and a chorus of birds singing joyously.

The focal point of their living room, the majestic grand piano, was rolled aside. Kathy arranged for a rented hospital bed to be placed in the former piano space, facing the all-encompassing view. With the head of the bed raised, Barb could absorb the power of sunlight and swarm of living creatures. As she sat facing the glorious sunrise, the golden hues warmed her face, now continuously growing taut and gray as life was waning. It was as if that bright ball of energy was determined to pass its energy in order to replenish her life force; indeed it appeared that way as the beams of light brightened and added pinkish-peachy tones to her skin.

Barb had been a nurse for years, caring for many sick and dying. Kathy was studying at seminary, and as part of the curriculum she was finishing a course in clinical pastoral education (chaplaincy). Both Kathy and Barb knew the significance of caring conversations. But they were sisters. They were young, both in their fifties. They did not want to have caring conversations…it did not seem right. It did not seem fair. Yet they knew the conversations were too vital to Barb's transition and Kathy's grief to forgo. Heart-rendering, tearful, laughter-dotted, caring conversations took place between Kathy and Barb. Kathy also helped facilitate an open door to her home so that caring conversations could take place between Barb and her children, her nurse co-workers, and other loved ones. Kathy was present to sit with her sister, to listen to her sister's expression of anger, sadness, joyful memories, and love. Sometimes Kathy just sat to the side of the hospital bed, never saying a word, both she and Barb content to be in each other's presence.

Kathy was also present at the moment of her sister's passing. Kathy had witnessed people at death's doorstep or immediately following death as part of her chaplain training and hospice volunteer work. But she had never been present at the instant of a person's last breath and release of soul–much less that of her only sister. Yet she did not cower from the thought that it may be too traumatic, too gory, or would leave a scar in her memory.

As Barb released her last breath, Kathy stood at her sister's bedside. She gathered her sister's body close to her own, tears streaming as she burrowed her face in the close embrace. Kathy gently laid her sister's body back against the pillows and looked upon her sister's face. Kathy blinked hard to clear the tears…could what she saw be true? If it was real then it was a miraculous phenomenon! In the moments following death, a smile had appeared on Barb's face! Yes, a smile that said "Everything is wonderful now!" replaced the struggle of the past several months. Kathy cried out to her husband, "Look! Look!" Her husband David and others who visited soon after her passing witnessed Barb's peaceful smile.

Although Kathy's heart is heavy with loss of the earthly presence of her most endeared family members, it brings her comfort and reassurance to think of the smile on Barb's face. It took a lot of courage for Kathy to fight along beside her sister, through pain, loss of bodily function, and fear that death might come. Many people are afraid to witness death. Kathy found the courage to perform the difficult task of helping her sister transition out of this life. She unquestioningly moved forward with that courage because she loved her sister. She believed there was no better way to *honor* her sister's *life* and ***honor*** her sister's *death* than to help her be physically comfortable while helping her resolve the legal, physical, emotional, and spiritual aspects of her life.

The gift in this endeavor for Kathy was Barb's smile. From Barb's smile comes Kathy's belief that her sister, brothers and mother are at peace and happy. I believe the smile was Barb's way of saying, "Hey, sis…this is great! I am at peace. Thanks for all you did to get me here as peacefully and easily as possible!"

There were times during her sister's illness that I talked on the phone with Kathy every day. I know there were days that were as agonizing to Kathy emotionally as they were to her sister physically. On one occasion, Kathy really, *really* wanted her sister to try a proposed medical treatment. Barb firmly had decided against trying another treatment. Kathy respected her sister's decision…and let go. How is that for love so unconditional it put a loved one's last wishes before her own strong desire? An opposite but equally agonizing scenario occurred when Kathy believed the surgery her sister had decided on would have greater physical trauma than it would have physical benefit. Kathy respected her sister's desire and hopes…and backed off. Again, Kathy was a remarkable example of unselfishly respecting a loved one's end-of-life wishes.

Kathy is one of the smartest attorneys I know. She is also one of the most selfless and intuitive people I know. As an attorney Kathy fully understands the legal doctrine of "informed consent." In the medico-legal realm informed consent means that every competent adult has the right to request and REFUSE medical treatment. Barb was a nurse. As a nurse she knew the medical treatment options available to her as well as their risks. Informed consent provided her with the legal right to know about and request medical treatment options. Informed consent also provides each competent adult the right to say "no" to any medical treatment offered to them.

During the hours of testimony from people during the Michigan Senate assisted suicide hearings and the Michigan Commission on End of Life Care, I became deeply troubled by the number of statements I heard from people who wanted the ability to bring about their death out of fear because they did not want to be "forced to be kept artificially alive by machines for years." I was distressed because these individuals wanted to shorten their lives for a reason that does not exist! It is well established law that you cannot be forced to be kept artificially alive. You even have the legal ability to preserve your right to request or refuse medical treatment after you become incompetent. To preserve that right you simply have to write out an advance directive. As it sounds, an advance directive allows you to direct others about your health care wishes in advance of you becoming incompetent and needing health care. Advance directives come in many forms: living will, power of attorney for health care, and the Five Wishes form. Michigan law permits you to designate a patient advocate who can make health care decisions for you in the event you are physically or mentally unable to make those decisions. Most advance directives do not require the use of an attorney to complete them. They are official when you sign them and have witnesses sign that you were competent when you signed. Most advance directives do not require a notary and do not have to be filed with the court. Free, relatively simple forms that ask you to check or fill in pre-typed boxes are available through your local hospice, hospital, church, or legislator.

Kathy's legal background told her that Barb had the right to refuse the medical treatment option offered her and the right to know about and request the surgery. Kathy's intuition told her that it provided Barb a sense of control over her situation to refuse the medical treatment option and a sense of hope to pursue the surgery option. It was Kathy's extraordinary selflessness to respect her sister's wishes that allowed her to do so without argument, or guilt manipulation.

Kathy–as do I—always has several projects going at the same time. Recently I tried to squeeze a call in to her on a mid-week evening around 9 p.m. I told her I would call her back when she said she was just walking out the door to help a person with cancer fill out their power of attorney for health care forms.

"But Kath…it is already late at night."

"I know it's late but the person recently learned of the end-of-life situation. This was the time the family can fit it in."

Yes, this is my friend Kathy. Volunteering to help someone start the process of completing the end of his life, despite the fact that it was late in the evening, and she had to work and attend her Master of Divinity classes the next day. I tried to call her back a few days later during a twenty minute drive. As I told Kathy I had reached my destination I chuckled as I realized I had left work to assist an aging couple with concerns they had with their previously designated patient advocate forms. Both Kathy and I understand the peace of mind that comes from taking charge of your health care desires. We also understand that it can be intimidating and sometimes scary to think about your own death. The thought of losing a life-long companion may be even more frightening. It takes a lot of courage to honestly deal with the fact that you will die. It also takes a lot of courage to sit with a person who is dying. Minutes, maybe hours may go by without a word being said. But it is your presence that brings peace and transfers love to the dying person. It takes a lot of courage to face the spouse or child of a person who is dying. But it is your long hug, your unconditional listening that helps a person feel at ease to allow tears to flow and express a full range of emotions, which brings comfort and lends strength to the loved one.

You may think you could not sit with a person who is dying.

"I would not know what to say."

"I am not good with sickness."

"I become faint around medical issues."

You may believe it is too uncomfortable to be around the spouse or child of a dying person.

"I don't know what to say to make them feel better."

"I can't stand to see people cry."

When I am about to enter the hospital room or home of a person who is dying, and I start to have feelings of anxiety or dread, I redirect my thoughts to the fact that the focus of the visit is not about me. The focus is about the dying person and loved ones. I breathe in assured tranquility as I recollect that my presence will hopefully bring some type of serenity, relief, or love. To avoid the situation because I might feel uncomfortable quashes the opportunity to convey peace, relief, or love to one of the most important aspects of life.

Kathy and I consider it a privilege to possess the legal knowledge of and personal experience with how to bring peace of mind, love and even joy to the end-of-life. We believe that with the privilege comes the duty to help others plan a peaceful and love-filled end-of-life. Advance care planning is a way we honor the end of the cycle of life. Sitting with a person who is soon to pass from this world or holding the sobbing loved one is a way we honor the end-of-life. You may worry that you will not know the right words to say to someone who is dying or someone who just lost a loved one. But often no words are needed. Rather it is your human presence, your holding a hand, your steady embrace that transfers warmth and reassures that someone is there who cares. It is the way we might help a person find the courage to bring peace and love, to the last days of their earthly life or to the earthly end of the person they love so dearly.

It takes courage:

- To think about and execute your own advance care planning.
- To help your loved one formulate their own advance care planning.
- To touch those who are sick.
- To look into the eyes of someone whose face is deformed by disability and smile back so she may receive some of the warmth of your smile.
- To leave your comfort behind and sit at the bedside of someone who is soon to die or hug the loved one who will soon experience loss.

Chapter 6
Living Life with Coraggio While Facing Death

Karen and I were classmates through all three years of law school. Karen's striking blue eyes, quick legal mind, and phenomenal public speaking ability were enviable. We were a part of a group of friends bonded by the hell fires of law school. Our group continued to keep in touch more than a decade after law school.

Karen's breast cancer diagnosis occurred at the time I was undergoing several years of ankle fusions and replacements. I did not see her for most of her surgery and treatment but our mutual friend, Donna, kept me updated on her health.

The first and second Coraggio books were published and this book had been written when Karen told me her cancer had returned. After several chemo rounds Karen let me know her cancer was "Stage IV." She explained that she wanted to spend her time helping other people get through cancer treatment. I was deeply moved by Karen's spirit, although her days might be quickly running out, she wanted to use them not for herself—but to help other people. The flash went through my mind later that night. Karen's generous spirit would have a voice, and Coraggio! Honoring the End of Life would reveal the perspective of a remarkable person living life with coraggio while facing death. Enough words from me. Here are the inspiring words written by my brave friend:

Karen's Story

December 24, 2009. I should have known something was wrong when the MRI technician was a little too nice, even for Christmas.

"Do you have a ride home, Mrs. Pilat?" *Why would I need a ride home from an MRI? Chemotherapy? Yes. Radiation? Yes. MRI...?*

"No. I can drive myself. I am going right home."

Except "right home" this day was not a direct route. After leaving the MRI, I went as far as the driveway to my home to pick up my husband, Mark. Before my mother-in-law arrived at our house to make the annual trek to my sister-in-law's house for her Christmas Eve-birthday dinner, Mark and I had to pick up hot hors d'oeuves at Hiller's Market, and our year-old Malti-pom puppy from her "bath 'n brush". We were almost home when my cell phone rang.

"Karen. Where are you and why don't we have the right phone number to get ahold of you?"

"Who is this?"

"It's Dr. P. I need you to go to Beaumont Emergency immediately."

"Can I go after dinner at my sister-in-law's? It is her birthday today and…"

"No, Your C-5 (cervical spine vertebra #5) is fractured and there is a tumor on your spinal cord…."

At that point, my world became one of images. Tears were running down my face while doors were being slammed.

The word "surgery" stuck in my brain while I waded through groceries strewn on the kitchen floor. Mark had fallen into a fetal position and was cursing God. "He's done nothing for us," Mark ranted in-between hyperventilating breaths. My mother-in-law arrived in our living room and was holding trash bags of Christmas gifts while sobbing and saying "Oh, no."

Mark and I had recently talked about how well we thought I was when Dr. P. called. My health wasn't perfect. I had been suffering from unexplained shoulder pain for months before my Christmas Eve MRI. On the plus side, in five years, I had been to hell and back but lived to tell about it: a breast cancer diagnosis a year after life-saving open-heart surgery to fix a congenital heart defect, a double mastectomy and two reconstructive surgeries due to the quick build-up of scar tissue, months of hairless chemotherapy with years of bald Christmases, removal of my ovaries and any chance that I would have children, back and leg surgeries when cancer recurred and destroyed vertebrae and my left femur, weeks of radiation that opened up my skin like miniature volcanoes, months in physical therapy re-learning how to walk, and years on the wrong drugs or unmonitored chemotherapy drugs that would cause me to have a mini-stroke and congestive heart failure in less than a year between the two events. But in my mind and what I told others about being 41-years-old with cancer: I was the luckiest woman alive!

To smile while you are fighting cancer

It was this inability to be defeated by cancer that defined my life with a terminal illness. I was and am the textbook definition of courage: "the attitude of facing and dealing with anything recognized as dangerous, difficult, or painful, instead of withdrawing from it." *Webster's New World Dictionary*, 4th Ed (1999).

I had not chosen to live my life with courage and smile through cancer as much as I had benefited from having relatives who were themselves examples of courage and did not let their circumstances dictate how they would survive whatever had befallen them. They just got through it with a smile on their face.

Like *Leeza's* Nagymama, I saw courage in action in my relationship with my maternal grandmother, Babcia (Polish for "grandmother"). Babcia had come to the United States from Bialystok, Poland in 1927 with no experience speaking or writing English and one relative living in the United States, my Uncle Jack. He paid Babcia's ship fare to New York City and her bus fare to Detroit so she could avoid an arranged marriage with the local shoemaker back home. Despite not speaking English or having a relative to help her out with more than fares, somehow, Babcia landed a job in a factory in Detroit attaching filters to the tips of cigarettes. An old maid at age 26, Babcia met and married my *Dziadzia* (Polish for "grandfather") in 1935 and had three children, my Auntie Titi, my mom, and my Uncle Joey.

Though I knew about Babcia's ziplock bag of medications that she took every day, it wasn't until the summer of 1974 that I discovered my beloved Babcia suffered on and off from strokes due to a weak heart and uncontrollable blood pressure. I only learned this after being appointed by my mom and dad, Auntie Titi and Uncle Joey to be Dziadzia's assistant in caring for Babcia, who had come home from the hospital after a stroke too weak to walk. Though she couldn't walk, Babcia retained her feistiness in her five-foot frame and gave verbal orders that her household be run and her family be cared for just as if she was well. Babcia could speak enough broken English, or I could understand enough Polish, so she could give me a list of tasks to be completed each day. Though she was bedridden for most of the summer and setback by another stroke while I cared for her, Babcia required that the windows of her Detroit ranch home be cleaned every morning. A streak of water or a speck of soot appeared and that set of windows was an automatic redo. While I was not charged with giving Babcia a daily bath due to her modesty in showing her "private places" to me, her ten-year-old granddaughter, I was asked to make all of her meals and make sure her body and clothing were remained clean afterward.

Because she had learned English from soap operas, every weekday from 12:30 p.m. until 4:00 p.m. I had the strangest task of watching her "stories", and telling her in detail what happened to Jill and Philip on "The Young and the Restless" and Bob and Kim on "As the World Turns" among other characters she liked or liked to hate because of their immorality.

I know from my own mini-stroke that my Babcia must have been very sick that summer, but she never complained about how she felt. Later, when she had carotid artery surgery and had staples visible in her neck, Babcia never complained about the pain or how gruesome the scars on her neck looked. Even when she was in and out of the hospital with congestive heart failure, which I have also suffered since having cancer, Babcia never complained about any of it. Why? It was because Babcia was too busy getting through her illnesses and surgeries, and onto recovery and living to be bothered with complaining, which may have slowed her down and kept her farther away from what she really loved to do—be with her family.

If Babcia was my first example of courage in action, my father, Mike, was my daily role model of handling pain and suffering with courage. Barely three years after I returned from my summer with Babcia, my father was diagnosed with adult onset diabetes. He had succumbed to his family history of diabetes despite exercising every day and watching his diet. Every adult in my dad's birth family had diabetes by age 40 and suffered tremendous consequences from it, from bleeding behind the eyes to no feeling in the legs. If a lifetime of diabetes wasn't suffering enough, my dad found out after his diabetes diagnosis that childhood scarlet fever had narrowed his mitral valve to the size of a swizzle stick and he would have to undergo open heart surgery to live beyond age 50. I will forever remember the smell and sight of my father after lifesaving valve replacement surgery: he smelled like the formaldehyde used to preserve fetal pigs upon which high school students could practice surgery and looked like a bloated Superman, with his chest puffed out and displaying a cross from which the surgeon opened my dad to save his life.

Shortly after heart surgery, my father realized something was wrong with his legs. That "something" was worn cartilage that resulted in bone-on-bone joint movement. For years, my father was walking on knees that had no shock absorbers. In the spring and summer of 2001, my dad had back-to-back knee replacement surgeries. From all of my father's illnesses and surgeries since age 40, the lesson in courage he taught me besides reinforcing Babcia's example of not complaining about pain and suffering,was to do whatever it took to get well. If you were required to get up and walk the high school track every day to rehabilitate your heart, do it. If you had to get your knees on a stretching machine twice a week in order to walk again, do it. If you had to "go to the House of Pain" (my father's reference to outpatient physical therapy centers) and work with a therapist to learn new ways of doing what you could do before surgery changed your way of getting in and out of a bathtub, do it. Babcia's "no complaining" combined with my father's "do what it takes" made it easy for me to exemplify courage and face and deal with anything difficult or painful instead of withdrawing from it.

Deep down, I was strong and at peace with fighting cancer because God had a plan for me. I truly believed and still believe that God was bringing me through each cancer horror because He wanted me to do something for Him to show everyone I met, whatever their faith, that God exists and He can change any situation. I did not focus on "Why me?" I concentrated on the fact that no matter what happened, I was getting through it and God was there. He would not leave me.

Live your life as fully as possible "til God says its over"

Until my neck surgery on December 26, 2009, no doctor had ever discussed prognosis with me. Then again, in all fairness, I hadn't asked. The only time I came close was questioning my then-oncologist, Dr. W., during my chemotherapy regimen in the summer of 2008, how long he thought I would live. When he responded with the oncology standard of "five years," which is the amount of time that medical studies follow a cancer patient in treatment, my mother and brother, Mikey, who accompanied me to that appointment, left the room gagging on their tears.

I heard the word "prognosis" for the first time after my spine surgeon, Dr. P., demanded that an oncologist talk to me about the prognosis for my cancer when he completed my neck surgery. After telling me that all he could do for me was replace cervical vertebra #5 because the spinal cord tumor was "vascular" (attached to the blood vessels servicing my head), Dr. P. told me that he could no longer "chase cancer all over" my body. Sometime after I heard Dr. P. say, "Nine months." *OMG. With only nine months of life left, I wouldn't make it to my 47th birthday on September 23, 2010!*

A week later my oncologist, Dr. Z., stopped by my hospital room to tell me he wasn't a fortuneteller. As my mother-in-law had said since my March 25, 2005 breast cancer diagnosis, "Who are you going to believe? God's Word, or man's claims about how long you will live?" Only God knew how long I was going to live.

After weeks of radiation had failed to shrink the tumor on the spinal cord in my neck, and cancerous lesions appeared in my lung and liver, Dr. Z. finally shined up his crystal ball.

"I am not concerned about the spots in your lung and liver. They are small. What I am concerned about is that the tumor on your spinal cord will snap your neck and you'll wind up a quadriplegic." *Quadriplegic? Really? After watching me suffer from cancer hell for five years, my 71-year-old mother is now going to visit me in a nursing home while I live life as a quadriplegic? No way. Unacceptable.*

If being told of the likelihood you are going to be a quadriplegic is not enough, Dr. Z. added that I only had six months left to live if I didn't immediately undergo aggressive chemotherapy. Three weeks on and one week off of Ixempra, the newest chemotherapy wonder drug to treat metastatic breast cancer (my diagnosis since February 2008), was what I hoped would get me to my birthday, now six months away, and beyond, God willing.

If you are depending on chemotherapy to prolong your life, what do you do about living? *I wasn't relying on chemotherapy to save me. I was depending on God.*

Heal relationships and Prepare for the end of life

In the meantime, I would juggle living with chemotherapy while preparing for death. For the first time in my war on cancer, I went on short-term disability leave from my employment as an attorney. I went back to my psychiatrist, Dr. L., who had listened to my fears about never being able to work again after back and leg surgeries in February 2008. I now needed her to help me with "end of life" issues, including coping with my husband's wholesale denial of my prognosis. I knew that my husband loved me and could not fathom his life without me, but his unequivocal denial that I was terminally ill hindered me from being able to process my feelings about dying and prepare for my own possibly impending death.

I started thinking about whom to give the modest assets that I had acquired in my 46 years, from my 2007 Ford Escape, to the box of silver dollars that Babcia gave me for my 16th birthday, to the Wedgewood china place settings I received as wedding gifts. I began planning my funeral. *Lynch Funeral Home, Catholic Mass at St. Kenneth's Church, funeral lunch with an open Margarita bar at El Nibble Nook....*

Despite the feeling that I was looking at death in my rear view window, I began living with the help of alternative medicine in February 2010. Although I did not know if those infusions were slowing my cancer growth, I felt better after I had a weekly or even monthly Vitamin C infusion while undergoing radiation and chemotherapy

The day before my 47th birthday, September 22, 2010, my oncology nurses suggested to Dr. Z. that I should be taken off of Ixempra. "She is just not the same Karen we know." I was still being assaulted by chemotherapy on an almost weekly basis. What suffered the most was my ability to communicate what I was thinking—or recalling anything to say at all. I had a bad case of "chemo brain," sometimes described by cancer patients as a "fog" in your brain. What I experienced in "chemo brain" was a long gap before I spoke where I struggled to remember what to say or failed to remember. This was particularly frightening for me, who spent 17 years as a trial attorney and relied on being quick on my feet. Not only my ability to communicate, but long periods of my life and education had been chemically peeled from my memory by chemotherapy. I couldn't remember anything from high school and reciting the Michigan Rules of Evidence by heart was no longer going to happen. I was a zombie but I did make it to my 47th birthday.

After five months of Ixempra infusions, in October 2010, I was scanned from head-to-toe to see if the latest wonder drug worked. The scans showed that although the small spots in my lung and liver had died, the tumor on my spinal cord had persisted. These were mixed results, but good enough get me off chemotherapy infusion and off short-term disability. On December 1, 2010, I returned to work as an attorney.

However, when every pill prescribed to me to stop the spread of my cancer made me so sick it hurt merely to touch my stomach, and the only infusion to allegedly stop the spread of my cancer, Herceptin, nearly killed me by causing congestive heart failure, Dr. Z. ordered a CT-scan of the chest, abdomen and pelvis and a complete MRI of the spine to check the status of my cancer. I would finish the tests one year after I had spent Christmas at Beaumont Hospital.

"I have read the results. You will have to tell my husband."

I wondered if my husband saw what I did on Dr. Z.'s face. "Karen's liver is covered with cancer, but it is still functioning."

"What percentage of my liver is covered?" *How did I go*

from zero liver tumors in October to tumors that covered my liver barely two months later?

"Too many lesions to count..." *Back to chemotherapy and short-term disability...*

"Will I make it to my 50th birthday?" My husband stormed out of Dr. Z.'s office with an "I am not going to listen to this." remark.

"No. And, if Halaven (the newest chemotherapy wonder drug) doesn't stop the spread and reduce the amount of cancer in your liver, you will only live, maybe, six months. I can tell you this because you won't dwell on it." *Don't they usually tell you to get your affairs in order at this point? Apparently not to an attorney...*

Instinctively, I began officially preparing to die while living my life—just in case, it was "my time." I appointed my brother, Mikey, as my patient advocate. Though your spouse is traditionally the patient advocate making medical decisions when you are unable, neither my husband nor my mother would be my patient advocate due to the emotional weight of deciding when to "pull the plug" on me.

As a result of latest six-month prognosis, I called a family meeting with my mother and my siblings, to be crystal clear about what my wishes were. *No tubes of any kind. No efforts to resuscitate. Hospice facility, not home. Cremation with a grave marker at St. Hedwig's Cemetery.*

While I was preparing to die while living courageously, I had forgotten what my planning for death might look like to the fly on the wall. Did I expect to die in 6 months (August 2011)? No. Did I want to die? No. Had I "given up?" No. It was just my training as an attorney. Prepare for the worst but expect the best.

It ain't over 'til God says it's over

I don't know when I am going to die. No one does. It's not our call.

The words still ring in my ears. "It ain't over 'til God says it's over." I believe everything happens for His reasons. I met a minister when I wound up in Beaumont Emergency for a leg infection after radiation. He never said a word to me until he passed my hospital bed, which was one in a corral of beds waiting for X-rays, and grabbed my hand.

"It ain't over 'til God says it's over," the minister said while squeezing my hand.

When I didn't respond, he urged, "It ain't over 'til God says it's over." With the fierceness of his belief staring me in the face, I felt tears run down my face. *Yes, it's God's call, not mine. I trust God with my prognosis.*

Besides Nonna's *Leeza*, the only person with whom I shared this encounter with the minister was Carole. In every group, there is the life of the party. In my Newly Diagnosed Breast Cancer Group, that person was Carole. She sat next to me in Beaumont's Rose Cancer Center conference room twice a week during the summer of 2005. During that time, including a notable joint support group with other cancer survivors and their significant others, Carole would take off her wig and swing it around her head like she was attempting to lasso a bull, merely to make us laugh or lighten the tone of the group.

Carole's breast cancer cruelly recurred six months after she had celebrated five years of being cancer-free. Carole thought she was forever done with cancer. Yet breast cancer had migrated with full force in her body to her bones and her brain.

In September 2010, Carole began the same dance I had been trotting with cancer and its treatment for the last three years: more chemotherapy and radiation until the cure for cancer came.

A survivor from our Newly Diagnosed Breast Cancer Group, sent me an email about Carole's progress. Channel 7 News had covered Carole's recent battle with cancer in a story, "Beaumont patient uses Skype to get to prayer service." In a link to the story, I heard Carole say: "I don't know how much time I have left…"

How did she know her time was "short?" How did anyone know when she is going to die?

I knew Carole needed to stop living like she was dying and return her prognosis to God's hands. Carole needed the message of hope that the minister had given me in the hospital bed corral. Because my blood levels were low (meaning I was susceptible to infection or could be an infection carrier myself), I sent a letter to Carole while she was hospitalized rather than visiting her, saying: "It ain't over 'til God says it's over." According to a fellow cancer survivor from our Newly Diagnosed Breast Cancer Group, Carole "appeared to draw a sense of hope and strength" from my letter. All I knew was Carole sang her sweet soprano in church barely a week after my letter lifted her up.

"It ain't over 'til God says it's over."

It takes courage to:

- Smile while you are fighting cancer.
- Trust God with your prognosis.
- Offer comfort and hope to others who have cancer or are caring for someone who has cancer.
- Heal relationships and prepare for the end of your life.
- Live your life as fully as possible "'til God says it's over."

Chapter 7

Dorme Bene, Bella Nonna

It is Italian *Tradizione* (Tradition) that the oldest granddaughter is sent to live with her widowed grandmother. So it was in Nonna's Southern Italian hometown of *Pedivigliano*. True to the Tradition, at six years of age Nonna moved in with her grandmother, a few steps down the narrow, dark, stone passage from her family's home. Nonna cherished living with her grandmother and proudly employed her role as grandmother's helper.

Nonna mentioned the Tradition repeatedly to me, her oldest granddaughter. I suppose Nonna believed the Tradition lived on through the 20th century and while desiring her oldest granddaughter to fulfill the Tradition, never wanted to pressure me. Nonna made an earnest attempt to understand the modern career-oriented, transient society. I did my best to fulfill Tradition's role. During school breaks and holidays I took up residence with Nonna. As her heart failure progressed I stayed with her most weekends.

Nonna was a voracious reader. Biographies, romance novels, historical fiction, and magazines; she read what came her way via friends and family. She read in bed before falling asleep. An early riser, she remained in bed and read until the sun came up. When overnighting at Nonna's, I was always last to bed. I inevitably attempted one more project before sleep: washing the last dishes in Nonna's sink, folding the clothes in Nonna's clean clothes basket, or returning a phone call to siblings who knew I had checked into Nonna's *cassa* for the weekend.

Before turning in for the night, it was customary to poke my head around her bedroom door to determine whether she continued absorbed in a romance novel. If she was awake and reading, as she typically was, I lay on the bed, curled at her feet. We talked for awhile, but when she sensed I was dropping off to sleep, her foot worked its way under the bedcovers to gently nudge me. I treasured our bedtime conversation, never wanting it to cease. But I had worked to exhaustion during the week and then raced for hours through traffic to reach her home. I knew my body needed eight hours of uninterrupted sleep.

I conceded to her nudging signal to head for bed in grandpa's bedroom. "Okay, *Bella Nonna*." (Okay, Beautiful Grandmother.) She was my beautiful grandmother, and with affection I addressed her so. With mischievous smile and arm-sweeping dramatic bow I backed out of her bedroom, lavishly adding, "*Princepessa*." (Princess.) Oh how I loved to hear the girlish giggle that erupted when I addressed her as *Princepessa*. Continuing to back away I stared at my Bella Nonna surrounded in her favorite color–lavender painted walls, lavender bedspread, and the lavender flowers she grew, dried, tied with a satin lavender ribbon and placed at her bedside in the purple cut glass vase. With lavender hue soft on her smiling face, against the lavender fabric head board, she always, *always*, had the last words "*Dorme bene*." (Sleep well.) I hear in my mind the loving way Nonna spoke the phrase to me. "***Door**-may **beh**-nay **Lee**-za*," with an accent of one whose first language was Italian. "*Dorme bene, Leeza*!" in the cheery tone of the ever-pleasant grandmother. "*Dorme bene, Leeza.*" with the sweetness of maternal love that warmed every bit of my being.

During the last years of Nonna's life, "*Dorme Bene*" took on a different meaning. It was the year 2000. The start of a new century. Nonna's 90 years of life had spanned almost the entire previous century. We stood in her backyard. Against the wire fence bordering her yard laid Nonna's garlic patch. Three feet deep and twelve feet in length, the tall, thin, antique-silvered dark-green stalks were densely packed. I bent over, grabbed a handful of stalks close to the roots and pulled. Pungent garlic odor immediately released and assaulted my nostrils. A few minutes earlier I had decided to help Nonna harvest her garlic crop. It involved pulling dozens of stalks until their prized, plump root bulbs loosed from the earth. This was not so good for my arthritic hands, wrists and elbows. My hands were already deformed into grotesque gnarls. My elbows were decrepit and, when inflamed, made it impossible to brush my teeth or hair, or lift an eating utensil to my mouth—basic every day activities not often thought of as involving elbow bending—but necessary to live. I was trying to take every precaution possible to avoid further elbow damage and thus avoid elbow joint replacements. I knew the garlic-pulling feat was a no-no. But with Nonna's advancing congestive heart disease, joint inflammation seemed the lesser of two evils. She could barely bend over and upright herself without fainting from impaired blood flow. Whether she acknowledged her advancing congestive heart disease did not matter: the reality of its limitations was apparent. Nonna was downhearted at the inability to pull her own garlic.

"Wow, Nonna! You have a great garlic crop this year!" I gushed, trying to boost her spirits. "Yes. Yes, *Leeza*. It was warm and wet this past month…that really helped the plants to grow." The warmth and humidity continued this autumn afternoon but the chilled breeze, scent of fallen leaves, and low angle of the orange-tinged sunlight across her back yard signaled that winter approached. Little did I know that this fading-sun, aromatic, end-of-season harvest would be the backdrop for conversation about the final season of Nonna's life.

I continued to bend and tug the bulbous treasure from its earthly hiding place. At least it had rained recently, making the earth fall away with more ease than usual. Nonna had gone ahead of me, snipping the seed-heads from the garlic stalks. Nonna was less than five feet in height and the garlic stalks having reached over two and a half feet in height, she needed not to bend at all to sever the seed-heads. She placed the decapitated heads in the old basket whose bowl and handle were made from woven willow branches. The willow branches, now grayed with age, reminded her of the baskets her father, Genaro, wove back in Italy. For that reason it was one of her favorite baskets, as she had mentioned on several occasions. The heads looked like an encased miniature bulb of garlic cloves. "Now…I save these and they are the seeds I plant for my garlic next year," Nonna explained as if I did not know the procedure that had taken place in her backyard for decades. She paused. She let the filled willow basket fall to the soft grass by my feet. Her sigh was telltale. Could she be wondering the same as me? *Will there be a garlic patch next year?* She leaned against the garden hoe/makeshift walking stick/makeshift support beam.

"You know, *Leeza*, when your grandfather and I first moved to this house, I used to walk to Mass every morning. After he would leave for work I walked to Jefferson Avenue and followed Jefferson to St. Lucy's Church. There was an old woman who walked along Jefferson to Mass every morning too. We ended up walking together many times. You know what that old lady told me she was going to Mass for? She told me she was going to Mass every day to pray for a good death." Nonna stopped talking.

I continued pulling garlic bulbs from their nestle in the rich earth. I was in listening mode and only murmured, "Oh my."

"Yes, *Leeza*. She told me she was praying for a good death." Again, she stopped, then restarted again in almost a whisper. "I thought she was gruesome. I mean I thought… this woman is really strange. *Leeza*, I thought she was really gruesome." Nonna always pronounced the word gruesome in an exaggerated manner, befitting to its meaning, with a rolling "r" and a drawn-out "ew", sounding similar to "grrrr-eeeeww-some".

"But now I know what she meant…I understand now what she meant about praying for a good death, *Leeza*." Her voice dropped to a whisper again toward the end of the last sentence. We were not making eye contact. My eyes were focused on the stalks in hand and the many, many more yet to do–the rows seemed never to end. Her eyes were also focused on the pulling project. I said nothing again, wanting only to be present to listen. I mumbled "hmmmm" so she would know I was following her and as oddly as the story was unfolding, that it was okay to continue.

"I am praying for a good death…that my death may be peaceful. That I go to sleep and peacefully pass into heaven to be with grandpa…and my daughter…and my mother."

I did not stop Nonna's talk. It was part of her end-of-life process. I did not try to negate her feelings by saying, "Don't be ridiculous, Nonna. You aren't going to die soon." Nonna had pondered her mortality. She was preparing for her transition from this life into the next. It is of paramount importance for people to complete relationships that have been interrupted, to make peace with themselves, to say "I love you!," to make peace with their divine maker, to make peace with death. And I would help Nonna with her end-of-life process; to bring to fruition the vital messages:

"I forgive you."

"Please forgive me."

"I love you."

"Thank you."

"Goodbye."

And I could start right now by listening as she sorted

through the blend of love-of-life courageous determination to stay alive versus the courageous realistic contemplation of determination on how to live her final days: to accomplish before dying a peace with herself, with loved ones and with her Divine Maker; to accomplish in death to be with her loved ones already passed and to meet her Divine Maker.

Nonna had already started sorting through her worldly possessions. I had discovered names of family members written on small squares of masking tape adhered to the backs of heavier objects and the bottoms of tea cups, or snippets of scrap paper slipped into zipper-locked plastic bags holding hand embroidered hankies or doilies. As she got further along into her sorting process, or perhaps more aptly named "serenity process," she reminded me of post-death possession designations such as, "Now don't forget *Leeza*, this goes to your father…it was his grandfather's and his grandfather adored him." She gained deeper inner peace through acting on her desire for a good death; resolving critical aspects of her life the best she was able at the time, and giving treasured material objects to people it was meaningful for her to know would possess them.

Nonna also began directing us how to achieve her ideal good death:

> "Nancy, this is the pink dress I want to be buried in and here is where you can find it. This is my special Rosary…the one I got when I was in Rome…make sure they put this one in my casket."
>
> "Paul, you are in charge of everything as soon as I go. Keep a copy of my will where you can find it so you can start with my wishes as soon as I die."
>
> "*Leeza*, I want to be able to breathe no matter what. Don't let them put that no revive thing (do not resuscitate order) in my chart so they give me oxygen if I can't breathe."

> "Pasquale, you know I have to be laid out at Bagnasco Funeral Home. That is where your father was laid out. Of course I have to be laid out there too..."

To participate in each aspect of a loved one's end-of-life transition, independently or collectively, is an honor. Whether it is in healing your relationship with that person, arranging good comfort care, or assisting in settling legal and financial affairs, each "piece" helps to achieve the other "peace" that leads to a good death.

I do not regret one minute I spent with Nonna. Bereft of the opportunity to tell my mom I loved her before she was unexpectedly killed, I knew the importance of saying goodbye, of having the "caring conversations" to fulfill the "Let's forgive each other"...the "I Love Yous"...the "Thank yous"...the "Goodbyes." Our society has an obsession with youthfulness magnified by a fear of death. The fear causes many to shrink away from a person who is dying, but I truly believe there is no more honorable privilege than to help a person transition from this life to the next.

For all the pain and struggle of having to face two serious illnesses and the sudden loss of my mother and maternal grandmother before the age of twenty-five, there were beneficial aspects of those cruel lessons. The harshness of those situations forced me to stare my mortality and the mortality of the people with whom I loved the most, squarely in the eye. I was toe to toe with the grim reaper, staring into the faceless, cold, blackness beneath his hood. Acceptance of the possibility of my own death was much easier than even the thought of losing my mother and maternal grandmother.

My Italian grandfather died from pancreatic cancer in 1978. I was a seventeen year-old filled with teen drama and rebellion. My grandfather had a thick Italian accent, loud voice and passion for people, food and his homemade wine. His end-of-life story occurred in a time when the patient was not told he had a terminal illness. The patient would undergo an "exploratory" surgery. During the surgery parts of their organs and tissues would be removed. After the surgery the physician would enter the room, escort the spouse, son or daughter into a private room separate from the patient and tell the family they had diagnosed cancer, there were or were not any treatment options and the patient had an estimated number of months to live. The family would reenter the patient's room with eyes puffy and nose red from crying yet pretend that everything would be okay. Then the patient, seeing the devastated looks of his loved ones, in turn would pretend that he didn't know he was dying. And the charade would continue. In my grandfather's case, my big ears radar tuned into Nonna and my father speaking in hushed tones. The radar acuity "mistakenly overheard" the phrase "*...his cancer.*" With teenage righteousness the size to match the big ears radar, I confronted Nonna and my father for the truth about whether grandpa had cancer. I, of course, was chastised for "deliberate overhearing." The chastisement was minor in comparison to the stern warning, "Don't tell Grandpa!" How odd. Here was a large, loud, strong Italian man, and no one would tell him he had cancer; no one would gently explain he would die soon. But this "Don't tell the patient the bad news" left the patient with no ability to make a decision on whether to or how to treat the cancer. Even more deleterious with this approach is the loss of ability to work through the relationships with oneself, with God, and with others. The charade robs a person of the caring conversations:

"I forgive you."

"Please forgive me."

"I love you."

"Thank you."

"Good-bye."

The crisp, sweet-smelling spring of 2003 was moving into the oppressive muggy feel of a Michigan summer. Even more oppressive was the news that Nonna was back in the hospital. The nasty fluid build-up of end stage heart and kidney disease was cycling more rapidly now. It seemed that Nonna had to be hospitalized every several weeks to artificially remove the fluids from her body that her failing heart and kidney could no longer eliminate. I was only six months into my administrative law judge position. Being the employee with the least seniority meant less complex but higher volume of cases scheduled per day. Add to that scenario that one of the three administrative law judges in our office was absent on indefinite sick leave, and the result was eight to nine hearings scheduled for my docket each day.

This particular day was beyond hectic. I had nine administrative hearings scheduled for the day and, unmercifully, none of the cases adjourned or had to be dismissed. That meant I had hearings scheduled to begin at least every hour. Between two hearings I received an urgent message left by my sister. Nonna's hospital staff had informed the family that Nonna's kidneys had almost completely shut down. Apparently the staff reached that conclusion because eight hours after placing a catheter into Nonna's bladder, barely any urine had appeared in the clear plastic window of the urine catch bag. I know Nonna's doctors had to increase the amount of diuretic necessary to remove fluid at each hospitalization, but it seemed strange to me that the kidney shut-down process wouldn't be more gradual. I had been holding off on having my good-bye talk with Nonna. I had soul-deep love and appreciation I wanted to express while she could look in my eyes, but I knew Nonna. She was intuitive, she was smart. I had made an unspoken pact to help her battle the congestive heart failure until the end. I had held off on the "good-bye" talk fearing she would think that I had given up on her. But I was anxious she might slip away before I could tell her she meant everything to me. For more than a dozen years, the festering boil of regret at not telling my mother of my love for her had inflicted its prickly sting. I struggled intensely and prayed fervently to know when to say goodbye to Nonna. Nonna and I were a formidable force and fought together for years to cheat death. Up to this point we had always been victorious! Now, this day, when I heard the medical personnel believed she had only one to four days to live once the kidneys shut down, I decided the farewell talk could not wait any longer.

My instant reaction to hearing the kidney-shut-down news was to leave work as soon as I finished my nine hearings and rush from Lansing directly to St. John's Hospital in Detroit to be at Nonna's side. That meant I would have to forgo the Italian American Bar Association of Michigan Justinian Night. Each year the Italian American Bar Association of Michigan honored the Italian-American judges, and as a new administrative law judge I had been invited as one of the judges to be honored. In the more recent years, as Nonna become increasingly unable to get out into the community, I tried to bring the world to her. I would try to think of some event each day that I could report to her. It might be a national event I heard on National Public Radio as I got ready for work in the morning: Pope John Paul II had presided at an event organized by the Vatican to signify the beatification of Mother Teresa. *Nonna will love this story*. Or that international aid was rushing in to assist the earthquake victims in central Italy. *Nonna will click her tongue when I describe this event*. Nonna loved her family and I tried to tell every day a story of the humorous statement or action of one of her great-grandsons. *I can already hear Nonna chuckle with delight!* And always Nonna asked, and I told her, what molte bene food I had eaten or purchased.

"Oh it was a long piece of beautiful, fresh whitefish…like *bacala*…and for only $2.99 per pound! Nonna you wouldn't have believed how good it was…"

A special bonus was the story I took home from a restaurant. I was attentive to the ambiance, the wait staff, the food presentation, the quantity, the smells, and the flavors. I replayed it detail by detail to Nonna. Nonna thrived on these stories. We could go on for 15 to 20 minutes over the telling of one good meal: "The waiter spoke Italian, so I ordered all my food and drink in Italian!" Nonna loved that. "The eggplant parmesan was *molto delicioso* Nonna. The eggplant wasn't sliced too thick or too thin. The sauce was thick. You know I love thick, plentiful sauce. They didn't put all that fake mozzarella cheese over the top...you know I cringe at the American counterfeit blanketing of Italian food."

Nonna was all over these food stories. It transported her for a few minutes from her declining mobility and increasing isolation, to her rustic childhood table, surrounded by her parents, HER *nonna*, and her sisters...or to a booth in an authentic Italian restaurant...or seated next to the highchair where her great-grandson had finished an adult portion of "pa-sgetti" and sat smiling with a bright orange-red spaghetti sauce covered face! Nonna was thrilled! The food stories were second only to the family stories for the pleasure they brought to Nonna. The best stories—truly the gems among narratives—were the ones I could concoct that combined food with family, such as the spaghetti sauce-covered great-grandson!

In debating whether I should forgo Justinian Night 2003 and instead head straight to the hospital, I considered the daily storytelling ritual. If I attended even a portion of the event I could enter Nonna's hospital room replete with a treasure trove of Italian, judge, lawyer, and food stories. I might not have been able to fix her kidneys, but the trove of stories would be invaluable to raise Nonna's spirits! I drove furiously to make it from Lansing to the Sterling Heights Penna's Italian Banquet Center in time for the pre-meal reception and judges' commemorative photo in front of the restaurant's grand staircase. The photo taken, I waited until all the judges were introduced, then made a sincere apology for having to leave without eating, and slipped out of the dining room. As I started my car, dread heavily fell as I thought of the "good-bye" task that lay ahead.

It was about 7:45 p.m. when I hit Nonna's hospital room floor. I set my face with "I am important and know what I am doing, so do not stop me" to avoid being turned back due to the end of visitor hours. Most of the nursing staff were in the 7:00 p.m. change-of-shift report and I made it without question. I walked into the room, bent over Nonna and kissed her on both cheeks. Nonna and I always kissed on both cheeks, followed by a back-patting hug. Tonight it was difficult to configure a meaningful hug while Nonna lay in the hospital bed with an IV in one arm. I sat on the edge of the bed, close to the bend in the mattress that elevated her upper body so I could comfortably grasp her hands in mine as I spoke. Nonna's lips were stretched in two straight, tightly pressed lines. I could tell by Nonna's face and her subdued tone that she had learned her kidneys were no longer working. I tried to exchange lighthearted pleasantries but the woman with whom she shared a room still had visitors who were talking above the volume of the woman's television. Competing with the volume of the roommate, her visitors, the television, as well as Nonna's hearing loss was not very successful. With dramatic emphasis I shared all my fantastic stories of Justinian Night but they barely worked their planned charm; Nonna only slightly raised the corners of her mouth. What I really wanted was to check her urine catch bag. It was no use trying to hide my nervous energy any longer so I said loudly into one of her ears, "I hear you were not passing too much urine today." Nonna shook her head in affirmation. I impatiently rose and followed the tubing until I found the bag clipped to the bottom bar of the bed rail on the opposite side of the bed. I pushed back the bed sheets and held up the urine catch bag hoping… praying actually, to find clear golden fluid. Sure enough, there were only a few drops in the tubing. The catch bag was dry. Intuitively, it did not seem accurate to me that kidney shut-down would be so abrupt. We knew the kidneys were gradually failing as a result of the congestive heart failure and its treatments. But it only seemed logical to me that the kidney output would decline gradually also. For Nonna's kidneys to come to an immediate screeching halt from one day to the next was odd.

"Nonna. Do you feel like you have to pass urine?"

"Huh, *Leeza*? I can't hear you." "*Darn…she is not wearing her hearing aids*."

The roommate's visitors were leaving so the background noise continued, but I wanted to respect Nonna's privacy and not announce to the whole floor that Nonna was having urinary problems. Nonna had pride and I wanted her to be able to keep her dignity.

"Do you feel like you have to go to the bathroom?" I said more loudly, moving away from the urine bag so I could be closer to her ears and placing my hands over my lower belly hoping the mime would fill in for the words she might not hear. She got my question that time.

"Oh God, *Leeza*. It feels so full. It hurts real bad. I mean…it's gonna burst."

"Did you tell the nurse that it feels like you have to go to the bathroom?" It sounded like a silly question, but it was important.

"Yes. Yes. I told them a couple of times…starting this afternoon."

"What happened when you told them?"

"Well, one time they looked under the sheet and said everything looked fine…that it was just my kidneys…the other time they just shrugged their shoulders."

The hallway was clear so I sneaked a read of her chart. From my pre-med student's read I did not see kidney function lab results with high alerts indicated. The chart did reflect that there had been no output since her catheter had been placed at least 16 hours before. She had received at least 20 ounces of fluid via her IV from what I could tell. From what Nonna told me about what she had to drink that day, she had at least 18 more ounces of fluid. And yet there was only three drops of urine in her catheter tube and she was fully alert. It did not add up. At the risk of being asked to leave, I walked and asked assertively until I found her nurse. I explained that Nonna had had no output since placement of her catheter. "I know. I heard it in report." I asked the nurse if anyone had checked the placement of her catheter since it had been inserted. The nurse patiently explained she had just begun her shift and when the no output report was given there was no mention of any catheter placement problem. I could tell by the nurse's forced-patience tone that she was sending me a message:

"This is what happens when someone is actively dying, lady...Deal With It!"

Okay. Time for me to crank up the assertive mode to the Lisa the Judge-Attorney mode.

I politely but firmly pled with the nurse to at least check Nonna's catheter placement. The nurse stared at me and sighed. She appeared exhausted and frazzled even though she had just started her 12 hour shift. I am not sure whether it was her compassionate heart reaching out to my broken heart, or her weariness tired of my insistence, but the nurse agreed to examine Nonna's catheter placement after she checked some of the critical patients she had yet to assess.

It was already nearing 9:00 p.m. I had the 90-minute drive back to Lansing ahead of me. The first 45 minutes had the city freeway lights of metro-Detroit to guide me, but the latter 45 minutes were completely dark. The combination of dark, with the depth of exhaustion I felt, was unsettling. "Ug." I had another crammed schedule of hearings to face in the morning. The administrative law judge runs the show during the hearing and must be alert enough to gather proper evidence, and focused enough to hear each objection and make a split-second decisive ruling.

God help me. Please help me. I need your help now to know what to say to Nonna. I also need your help to get me home tonight and to have enough energy to function tomorrow. Oh please, dear God...

I took my usual seated position, a one hip/buttocks/thigh-stride on the edge of Nonna's hospital bed. I took her IV-free hand into both of my hands. The phlebotomists had such a difficult time in recent months trying to find a compliant vein to successfully draw blood for laboratory work that Nonna's beautiful hands were mostly black-purple and green from bruising. She was so depressed she wasn't saying a word or looking at me. This was not my Nonna. Nonna, in her matriarchal role, unceasingly offered encouragement to everyone. She consistently portrayed a positive attitude to all. Seeing her depressed added weight to my dismay. What could I possibly say to Nonna to adequately convey a lifelong culmination of love and gratitude? I was afraid to speak, sure from the tightness in my throat if I attempted any utterance an emotional sob would gush in its place. I was staring at her hand, stroking it gently while searching for the strength to speak.

My gaze transfixed on her hand as my tired mind wandered. In my mind's wandering the bloated and bruised hand became transformed into the strong hand I knew from youth. Those long beautiful fingers ending in perfectly shaped, thick fingernails. That beautiful hand holds a ball of cheesecloth, heavy with its precious treasure buried within. She unwraps the layers of cheesecloth, turning the contents over and over in her hand until the inner chunk is exposed. The paring knife fits perfectly in the palm of her hand. The blade resembles brushed metal now, after decades of sharpening by the gray stone at the side of the chipped, enamel sink. The knife's wood handle is now deeply grooved and flint-colored from the water-log of daily washing. The knife easily peels off the layer of soft greenish-blue fur to expose the golden translucent parmesan. The rich but pungent parmesan aroma reaches my nostrils at the same time she hands me the chunk she has cut for grating. Grating is delegated to grandchildren. It is risky, treacherous employment. Many the naïve child's knuckle has had skin sacrificed to the four-sided metal grater. It is a dreaded task for me, second only to standing at Nonna's kitchen sink cleaning raw calamari. I begrudgingly think of how my hands will carry the odor similar to acrid gym shoes for the next several days. Although immensely dreading the task, years of parental instruction about respecting elders prevents me from letting on. I know the meatball recipe from years of assisting and thus realize more grating is my fate.

Meatball production is a premeditated event. Days before, an unsliced loaf of dense Italian bread was purchased from Nino's bakery and left out to dry. I hear the sharp "crack" now as Nonna breaks the rock-hard oblong loaf in half, using the edge of the sink for leverage. She hands it to me for grating. Although large, the halved loaf feels weightless without its moisture. Nonna palms the paring knife again and clove after clove of garlic and stalks of Italian parsley from the garden fall in slices into the bowl. The savory smelling garlic and parsley pieces litter the top of a mound filling two-thirds of the bowl with ground beef, ground pork and raw eggs. Her strong hands fold in my mounds of grated cheese and breadcrumbs. Sometimes Nonna gathers up a baseball size portion of the mixture, flattens it between her palms to shape an oval, inserts one half of a hard-boiled egg and bakes it. On other occasions the mixture is mounded into a halved and scooped eggplant, drenched with thick, basic tomato sauce and baked.

But today the mixture is destined for meatballs to accompany spaghetti. In a matter of seconds she pinches off a sticky, golf ball-sized blob, rolls it between both palms and drops it into the heavy pan. Meatball after meatball is dropped into the sizzling pan. After browning on several sides, the meatballs are gently transported into the tall pot of sauce, belching in protest from the hours of heated boil. The fry pan again empty, the pinching, rolling hands deftly repeat the process until dozens of meatballs are prepared for the meal.

I am not sure whether it is Nonna stirring or the beeping from a hospital machine that brings me back from remembrance. I am still staring down at Nonna's hands. Cold, harsh reality crashes in. Nonna's hands are no longer the slender, hard-working tools of culinary and gardening wonder. They are purple and puffy again.

"Coraggio." Gather up your courage, Lisa. "Coraggio." Summon every bit of your emotional and physical strength.

There was no privacy; a woman with her mini-television

on semi-loud was a piece of hanging fabric away. I would have to speak loudly for Nonna, so that with her hearing loss she could understand every word I said. "Nonna" I said softly, but my voice cracked and my throat got so tight I was sure no other sounds could escape. I looked up at her. Oh, her face was beautiful, even through the body-failing puffiness, the striking, creamy skin and red hair remained. Her deep-set almond eyes were looking at me with profound love and sadness.

"Nonna, you have been such an important part of my life. You were my mother, my grandmother, my confidant, and friend. You have been my greatest cheerleader and even when I was accomplishing feats and thought no one noticed...you would tell me how proud you were of me. Nonna, because of you I have had...a wonderful life. Our story is a beautiful love story of a grandmother and granddaughter. I can never thank you for such an incredible gift. I...love you...*very* much, Nonna."

Phew. I had gotten through it without a major breakdown. Our eyes were locked together throughout my proclamation. I struggled now to grab a tissue to wipe my tears and nose without breaking eye contact or releasing her hand from my other hand. I was searching her face to see her reaction. I was worried she would be disappointed or upset. She didn't say anything for a few seconds. Ever so softly, with a tenderness of someone delicately retrieving an heirloom from an old trunk Nonna asked:

"*Leeza*, do you remember when you used to sit on my porch and sing songs in Italian? ...oh that was so good."

To be honest, I did not remember. Or maybe I vaguely could remember. Those insufferable mid-summer Michigan days when the heat and humidity were stifling. The escape was Nonna's red brick porch—overhang held by columns of filigree white iron—adjoining a matching red brick flower box overflowing with vibrant red geraniums. Yes, I sat many an hour with Nonna on that porch in hopes of catching any Lake St. Clair breeze. I was surprised that Nonna remembered me singing to her, most likely she joining in, the Italian *canzoni* (songs) I knew. I was also surprised that the songs and laughter we shared had been such a treasured moment for her. It was one of those classic examples of performing a simple deed and not knowing the positive, lasting impact it made on another person's life. Had I known it was such a coveted gem I would have given Nonna one hundred more Italian serenades.

But here we were in a crowded, sterile hospital room. Perhaps without another opportunity ever to serenade my sweet Nonna in her native language.

Nonna pulled her hand from its nestle between mine. She tenderly covered my disjointed fingers with her hand, gently pressing down into the white hospital bed sheets in a message of assurance while patting with matriarchal affection. She started to recall many of our family events that evidently held great significance for her. It was a life review of sorts, Italian-American style. Many people perform a life review in the days before they pass. Many of Nonna's reminiscent vignette's involved food, of course. About 45 minutes of "Do you remember…?" questions ensued, with me mostly nodding an affirmative and Nonna following her own question with the full story. She was orchestrating the review; a beautiful documentary of a giving, loving life, punctuated by her endearing chuckles and the corresponding grandmotherly pat on top of my hand. It was bittersweet. I laughed. I nodded. I gave expressions of exclamation. But all the time I could feel my heart ripping apart.

It was after 9 p.m. I had an hour and a half drive home and a long day of hearings a few hours from then. The drive was through an unsafe part of Detroit and then vast barren, dark farm fields with the threat of mating deer darting into the highway every foot of the drive. But I would not miss this retelling of Nonna's life with recollection of the moments held dear to her heart.

"Do you remember how much your father loved the stuffed artichokes? It used to take me all day to stuff each leaf with the bread crumbs and parmesan cheese. Oh...I would really jam the bread crumb and parmesan cheese in between the leaves!" Nonna would chuckle as if she had done something naughty...but good. "I used to call your father to come over. When he got there I would tell him to take home the big, heavy aluminum pot on the stove. When he lifted the lid and saw all those stuffed artichokes...his eyes bulged! Of course he took one out right away and ate it. I watched him. He scraped off every bit of the bread crumb and artichoke from each leaf with his teeth. Very careful he was...every little bit of each leaf." I could picture my father in my mind, elbows on the table, in good artichoke eating form, pulling through his clenched front teeth each one of Nonna's rich, sumptuous artichoke leaves." The thought caused me to utter an enthusiastic "Mmmmm."

"And your brother, Peter? Do you remember how much he loved the *Bistecche Impanate* (breaded steak)? Man, he used to devour a whole tray full." The "whole tray full" referred to by Nonna was a large heavy aluminum cookie sheet, piled three to four layers high with the parmesan-herb-breadcrumb-fried steaks. They were a highly coveted, savory delicacy in our family, my brothers stabbing and slicing into one steak after another. Nonna was motioning her head back and forth, as if in amazement of her grandson's passion for and ability to polish off piles of *Bistecche Impanate*. I mirrored Nonna's head motion in agreement with her amazement.

"And do you remember great-grandma Rizzo on Christmas Eve, by the stove frying the *grispelli*?" Some of my cousins called them *spingi*, a yeasted potato and flour doughnut, fried into rings or into a long, narrow shape filled with either a stick of *formaggio* (cheese) that would melt during the frying process or a full strip of anchovy. Yuck. My sister and I would shudder when we bit into the éclair shaped *grispelli*, hoping to find oozing warm imported Italian cheese hidden inside but instead having instant overpowering salty fish flavor, concentrated only as a canned anchovy is able, insult our taste buds! "**Ten pounds** of boiled potatoes, *Leeza*! **Ten**

pounds of flour *Leeza*! Can you believe it? And we would have to peel all those potatoes and force them through the ricer...all those ten pounds. Just for one recipe! The huge pan we had to use to allow it to rise. But everybody loved them. Your grandfather loved the one with the anchovy the best." Her head was moving side to side again, this time as if in disbelief that she and her aged mother could mix and fry the massive amount of heavy potato and flour dough each year.

"And do you remember Paul with the *zuppa di lumaca*?"

Lumaca...hmmm...what again was lumaca? I was exhausted. I couldn't think clearly...and for sure I could not remember the English translation of the word *lumaca*.

"Snail soup," Nonna responded to my quizzical look. "Your brother Paul was only three or four years old. We stood him on a chair next to the big pot. We gave him the long handled wooden spoon. We told him it was his job to make sure none of the snails escaped the pot. He was so serious and did a darn good job of hitting down any of the snails that crawled up the side of the pot to the top! He was so cute with that missing tooth!"

Nonna was chuckling so deeply now I could see her chest heave under the loose hospital gown. The corresponding pats on my hand were a merry staccato, in rhythm with her chuckles.

Wretched.

The snail soup was on my sister's and my most dreaded list; right up there with the seven Christmas Eve fishes, the black slimy mushrooms, and the puny, shriveled, baked squirrels. Snail soup was made of a thin tomato, garlic broth hiding chunks of potatoes and unspeakable, slithering, mollusks. The tomato broth and potatoes were not bad. My bowl of course also contained the unavoidable snails. Although I prayed that the soup ladle would miraculously miss any snail as it was scooped for my serving, the unmistakable clickety-clack against the ceramic bottom of my bowl as the steaming ladle tipped meant my snail-less prayers had not been answered. The steam cleared and before my bent, emotionless face appeared the now charcoal gray shells, as if the tips of icebergs, hiding slimy serpents below the surface. I mean snails. The snails you see crawling along the sidewalk, aided in locomotion by its own slime. Similar to brown-black slugs but these with the convenience of an attached coiled shell home. The snails for *zuppa di lumaca* were somewhat smaller than escargot, but not by much. Even though we were just children, a long, shiny metal snail pick was at our table setting, waiting for us to hook and yank the tough animal from its shell house. It amazes me that children these days command their parents what they will eat for dinner: a hot dog, french fries, chicken fingers, or a peanut butter and jelly sandwich. Yet there we sat... with NO option but to tug at the black elastic mollusk until it was loosed and then pray that its slimy quality would help it slip down our throats lest we bite into its rubbery and sometimes gritty body. A critical but cruel aspect of making *zuppa di lumaca* is the placing of live snails into the large pot of steaming broth. Hence follows a desperate attempt by snails to escape the pot and save their lives. And hence the important duty of little brother Paul, stood on a chair next to the stove, to stand guard with wooden spoon for any fleeing mollusks. Fledgling Paul was a cutey-pie...a sweet face with missing tooth after a toddler's trip on the front sidewalk. He did take his post with great seriousness; hitting furiously at any snail reaching the lip of the pot with a wooden spoon half his size.

"*Leeza*, your grandfather laughed so hard watching Paul he was crying. The snail soup story was one of his favorites," she reminded me. It was true. Paul and the snail soup pot was one of my grandfather's AND Nonna's favorite stories to tell.

O Dio (Oh God), how Nonna loved to bring us pleasure and express her fervent love for us through her marvelous, authentic food. I looked at her face. Her face had lightened throughout the 45 minutes and almost as many stories. She had a look in her eyes of pride, of satisfaction at almost a century rich in family, rich in tradition, rich in love and joyous moments. The light seemed to fade from her eyes as they fell upon our intermingled hands. She stopped patting the top of my hand. Reality had butted its ugly head into our beautiful life story. The life rich in family, rich in tradition, rich in love and joyous moments was coming to a close. *How could it be? Oh Lord. How could it be*? She was so lucid. She had the same inner zeal to selflessly serve her family as she had for decades. She wanted to forge ahead with us for decades to come. Her love for us was fueling a mighty will to live. She was facing death with the same powerful *testadura* (hard headedness) that carried her lifelong.

The 45 minutes of storytelling allowed the nurse to complete her shift-starting duties and as promised she returned to check Nonna's catheter placement. Indeed the catheter had been inserted incorrectly and her kidneys hadn't completely shut down after all. The hospital's erroneous blunder had sounded a false death alarm for Nonna and her family. In hindsight, the blunder provided a stage for a grandmother and granddaughter to review – hand clasped to hand – the beautiful love story they had created.

My resurgent hope was that she would be with us for a few more years, but it was only a couple weeks later, that a peaceful passing would prevail over Nonna's *testadura* spirit. Although early in summer, Saturday, June 21, 2003, started out sunny, hot, and sticky. The previous day Nonna had been discharged from the hospital to a nursing home. Her congestive heart failure had been repeating its wicked cycle. The cycle cannot revolve forever. The strain on the kidneys, first from the perceived weakened blood flow, next from the overreacting high blood pressure, and third from the strain of diuretics, was taking a mortal toll. Not only was Nonna in congestive heart failure, she was in end-stage renal failure. Nonna's nephrologist, cardiologist, and internal medicine doctor were wonderful to her. They knew Nonna wanted to continue treatment. Outside the presence of Nonna, we asked what "end stage" meant in Nonna's case. We asked her doctors if they had an estimate of how long Nonna had to live. We explained that we wanted hospice services for Nonna so she could receive palliative care and a peaceful passing. The doctors and nurses were reluctant to provide an estimate of time until her body would reach its final shutdown. We did learn that with congestive heart failure and end-stage renal failure death results from the human body no longer being able to filter all the toxins and fluids from the body. The toxins increase in the blood to the level where they actually damage the brain, resulting in coma and death.

Upon this latest hospital discharge however, the doctor did not agree to Nonna returning to her assisted-living apartment. During hospitalization the doctor had been reluctant to give a meaningful dose of diuretic because Nonna's kidneys had pretty much quit functioning. Enough fluid had been removed for Nonna to breathe a little easier, but she continued to be incredibly weak. Nonna was discharged to Bon Secours nursing facility a few blocks from my sister, Laura's house. Laura had been trying to encourage Nonna to eat but Nonna only was interested in getting back to her apartment. Because it was Saturday, I told Laura I would be at the nursing facility by lunch to see if I had any influence on cheering Nonna or encouraging her to take a little nourishment. Not only was it humidity season in Michigan, it was also "orange barrel" season. The shortened Michigan construction season meant that road construction was concentrated into a few warm months, June being one. I had moved into a condominium two weeks before. I dug through several unpacked boxes to find hot-weather clothes and managed to leave Lansing early enough to accommodate driving delays. But no matter which route I plotted I was obstructed by road closures and traffic. Exasperated, I watched the digital clock on my slow-moving car's console pass through the lunch hour.

I found Nonna in a wheelchair in the hall. In my panicked rush I almost passed her. "*Oh no. No God, no!*" Her beautifully shaped face, skin smooth even at 91 years, was puffy; a bloated distortion so drastic it appeared painful. I soothingly assured her we would make her comfortable. Slowly, as to not inflict even the slightest jar or bump, I wheeled her to her room. Miraculously my brother Paul appeared at my elbow. His lengthy, athletic arms effortlessly and gently picked up his endeared, petite Nonna and tenderly placed her in bed. We positioned soft pillows around, under and beside her for support and comfort. With Paul at her side I left the room and found the nurse and administrator, and we worked out a hospice plan. On Monday, when the proper paperwork and authorizations could be obtained, she would be transferred to the hospice wing. It was our goal for her to return home soon with hospice care.

When I returned to the room there was a shift in Nonna's look and communications. Her eyes looked foggy. Was it the toxins clouding her brain as her nurses and doctors had described? Already? Her beloved grandchildren Paul, Laura, and I were all gathered around her bed, in her line of vision, holding her hand or stroking her cheek. Her son Pasquale and her grandson Peter called and she heard their voices. We joked that Nonna was fighting with that darn *testadura* determination to stay with us. We vowed to reassure her it was "okay to go." We were all fine. She had given so much of herself to make sure we were fine. Her job had been completed...and with perfection. But her beloved husband, her endeared daughter and her adoring parents were waiting for her in heaven. It was time for her to be released from physical struggle and to join them. When Nonna would stir or moan the grandchildren circle-of-family-love we had formed around her bed would quietly assure her: "Everything is okay, Nonna." "We are all here, Nonna." "We love you, Nonna."

As the time neared 8 p.m. Laura leaned toward me whispering, "One of us should spend the night." That meant we would have to convince the nursing home staff to allow an overnight family member. Laura and I can be very persuasive. If the nursing facility staff acquiesced we would have to sit-sleep upright in the chair on Nonna's side of the room she was sharing with another patient. Laura and I were both exhausted.

Neither Laura nor I could bear to think of Nonna passing without one of us next to her. Yet again, no doctor would give us an estimate of when to expect death once a person's kidneys shut down and she refused to eat. A nurse friend told Laura it could be up to three days. With that knowledge I convinced Laura that it could be a long haul. I developed a plan for both of us to go home that night to achieve a restorative night of sleep. Rested, we would then take shifts, me staying through the first night, and Laura staying the next; repeating the shifts as necessary. Paul, Laura, and I prayed part of a Rosary sequence while encircling Nonna and left her beloved Rosary beads on the pillow to the right side of her face. Laura stayed and tucked Nonna in, ensuring she was as comfortable as humanly possible.

Back at Laura's house I tucked myself into the lower quarters of Laura's eight year-old son Michael's bunk bed. My eleven year-old nephew, Anthony, slept in the above bunk with the displaced Michael lying in his sleeping bag on the floor next to the bed. Ever the insomniac, I shoved ear plugs into my ears and buried my head under the pillow. The days of pushing physical limits overcame the traffic delay frustrations of the day and my worries about Nonna. I sensed Anthony turn over once in the bunk above me and was pulled into a deep and much-needed sleep.

A few minutes before 6 a.m. the door to my nephews' room slowly opened. The early summer sunshine, trying to burst through the narrow slits of curtain shading the bedroom window, shed enough light to make out the figures entering the room. I saw the silhouette of my sister…her husband, Mike, holding her from behind in a loving embrace. "Lisa." she whispered. From that one word I sensed she was crying. The upper bunk was so low that I couldn't sit upright in the bed. I struggled to maneuver my arthritic-stiff, adult body out from kid-sized lower bunk. "The nursing home just called. Nonna passed away in the night."

I shot out from the cubby-hole and stood upright, stomping my foot.

"No, no, no! I wanted to be there! I wanted you to be there! I wanted *someone* to be there…so she wouldn't die alone!"

Tremendous guilt pressed in. *How could you be so selfish as to seek sleep and abandon Nonna at the time of her death?* Tremendous self-disappointment brought a tightening to my chest.

Laura and Mike pulled me inside their warm embrace for a group hug.

"Lisa, you know Nonna. She never, *ever* wanted to bother us. This was her way…you *know* it."

Laura was right. I could hear Nonna's voice in my mind, "Youse girls just go along…I don't want to bother youse girls…," repeating the selfless phrases she had uttered on hundreds of occasions in the past. She had done it her way. For years she had prayed to pass peacefully in her sleep. The nurse said she checked around 3 a.m. and found our sweet Nonna, "sleeping more peacefully than she had at any time since she was admitted." When she checked again around 5 a.m., Nonna had passed. Nonna fought with *coraggio* and *testadura* until the very end…then peacefully transitioned to the next life.

Nonna, you spent a lifetime creating for me a beautiful love story between a grandmother and grand-daughter. Now it is time for you to Dorme Bene, Bella Nonna. (Sleep well, my beautiful grandmother.)

It takes courage:

- To change the things you can.
- To accept with serenity the things you cannot change.
- To fight to the end.
- To go in peace.

CHAPTER 8

Honoring the Legacy

Grieving the loss of someone you love hurts. Either I am not good at working through the grieving process or it is true you never get over it. But what I have learned to help the pain is to reflect on the person's legacy and take action to continue part of or the entire legacy. Ask: "What was his or her gift to my life?" How did he or she effect those around them? In what way did he or she contribute to the world?

Contemplate a way to perpetuate the legacy. Your actions keep the person's benevolence alive in the world while the person's love remains alive in your heart. Honoring a loved one's legacy is powerful! Not only do you continue to foster goodness to others, you also fill yourself with the warmth of his or her presence; a permeating warmth critical to soothe the void and ache of grief.

My mother's gift was being light and joy to all she encountered. The room brightened in her luminous presence. Spirits rose as they brushed against her vivacious aura. Hearts gladdened as she placed fingers on her ever-present guitar and burst into rapturous song. When my mother passed away I vowed to perpetuate her joyous spirit by beaming and singing to all I encountered. No matter how much arthritis pain I was experiencing or how weary I was from a pain-wracked, sleepless night, I tried to shift my focus to my mother's spirit of joy and strove to forward that light and joy to whomever crossed my path. I spontaneously burst into silly song to some people's dismay; intone an *Ave Maria* at funerals to the comfort of others. Her legacy is light, joy, and song. Perpetuating my mother's legacy helped me focus on positive thoughts about her life instead of the jarring reminder of loss.

My stepmother, Bonnie's, father owned the men's dress store in their small town of Harrow, Ontario, Canada. He knew everyone in town, and they knew his quick wit and the spark of his blue Scottish eyes. He was a church elder and Sunday school teacher. He cared about Harrow and took action to maintain its grand qualities. When her father died, the community planted a tree garden to memorialize his efforts to maintain Harrow and as a permanent memorializing gesture for all from Harrow who passed away that year.

It is common to hear that a financial trust was created to help the minor children of a parent that died or money was donated to a favorite cause in memory of someone who died. Being particular to persons with disabilities, I have noted that scholarships have been formed to assist a student struggling with the same illness experienced by the person who passed away. I am partial to rheumatoid arthritis and myasthenia gravis of course, and I am always humbled to read the tremendous impact on outreach and research made from the financial donations in memory of a person's passing. All of these actions are a way of perpetuating legacy. The perpetuation brings peace and gifts to the world.

Each Sunday Grandpa-Nonno loved to gather his family around him and a large table piled with savory homemade

Italian delicacies. Through Sunday Italian Family Feasts, he spread his boisterous demeanor, his stories of Calabria, Italy or his adventure of the week. His maintaining Sunday Italian Family Feasts solidified the importance of family and family values, and he passed the Italian heritage through the sharing of his dearly loved food, vino, and Italian music. It was extraordinary, the amount of love, bonding, passing of heritage, and important life lessons that were afforded at the Sunday Italian Family Feast. Nonno's generosity, vivacious participation in life, Italian heritage and love of family were his legacy.

Nonna recognized her husband's legacy. With a fervor she vowed to carry on his legacy of Sunday Italian Family Feasts. Once again, it was from courage that Nonna derived the determination to accomplish such a feat. As I think of it now, at her husband's passing, Nonna had never handled the household finances yet had to make due with a meager husband's pension and social security income, she had never learned to drive, and she alone had an entire house and garden to upkeep. The household upkeep and long hours of food preparation were all done on elderly, arthritic, and painful knees. I really do not know how Nonna obtained the incredible quality and quantity of food she used to prepare our Sunday Italian Family Feasts. Her knees were swollen to the size of small cantaloupes by then; there was no way she could walk to a grocer. She did not drive. Perhaps she gave a list to my father so he could shop before or after work, but I know she was reluctant to bother him—he being a single father of four teenagers, working the late night hours of a television producer/director at the CKLW broadcasting station in Windsor, Ontario. Perhaps she asked neighbors or visitors. I know that in her determination Nonna figured out how to use the St. Clair Shores City senior cab service for grocery shopping. For a simple, unsophisticated elderly woman to arrange a pick-up, payment, and return ride demonstrates her guts and her *testadura* determination to perpetuate the legacy. No matter the logistical and financial struggle to get foodstuffs or the physical struggles of feast preparation. Nonna was determined to carry on Sunday Italian Family Feasts after Nonno died. It was his legacy of love and family, and she honored his life by honoring his legacy. The Sunday Italian Family Feasts developed into Nonna's legacy–not just a legacy of family and love–but now expanded to a legacy of courage and determination.

It takes courage:

- To contemplate your legacy.
- To perpetuate the positive legacy of a loved one.

Chapter 9

Legacy Eulogy

My baby brother, Paul, is the family orator. He is "baby" in birth order only. He has maintained his 6'4" athlete's frame into his forties. Since he was a boy, he has commanded respect as a leader. He has used his attributes of good looks, unwavering principles, charisma, and positive attitude to inspire the people with whom he interacts, including the hundreds of girls and boys he has coached throughout the years. His magnetism, presence, strong voice, and eloquent command of speech honed from years of courtroom presentation make him a remarkable orator.

St. Lucy's Church, the parish where I was baptized into the Catholic faith, and where Nonna walked to daily Mass in the 1960s and 1970s, would host her Funeral Mass. The Pastor of St. Lucy's upheld the sanctity of the Catholic Funeral Mass and did not permit a non-ordained person to give a Eulogy as part of the religious ceremony. Respectful of Church dictate, Nonna's eulogy would be performed during the Rosary ceremony on the eve of her funeral.

Nonna's body had been placed in the largest viewing room of the Bagnasco & Calcaterra Funeral Home on Harper Avenue in Saint Clair Shores. "Of course," Nonna had previously affirmed when the subject had arisen about her funeral parlor preference. Her Italian husband had his viewing at this Italian-American purveyor of obsequies and thus it was presumed she would also. Bagnasco's was one of the Italian icons that forever graced Harper Avenue, as did Giglio's Italian meat store, Salvaggio's Italian fruit market, and Pete's Italian bakery—cultural beacons on the family car ride from our childhood home to Nonno's and Nonna's two miles away. We had passed the stately Bagnasco & Calcaterra Funeral Home hundreds of times, its two stories adorned with a flags on each side of the burgundy-colored fabric awning bearing the gold "B & C" insignia as if the entrance to an upscale big city hotel. Yet we did not pass by this time. Now, reluctantly, we turned our cars into the parking lot to pay respect to the 91 year-old matriarch of our Italian-American family.

The crowded viewing room was quieted for the saying of the Rosary, every chair occupied, a few visitors standing at the back of the room. From the podium to the right of Nonna's casket, the five decades of the Rosary were led, most of the present joining the recitation. Prayers were cast for the soul of Saveria Gigliotti. The room was silent and mood heavy as Paul, with upright, ceremonial posture, took his place behind the podium to face us.

"Nonna's life was dedicated to loving and serving her family."

Paul's rich, kind tone reflected his deep respect and love for Nonna. His words and delivery reminded each person in the room of the magnanimity of the love Nonna had for us. Tears started streaming from my eyes. I fought back sobs that were pushing to escape and turned my eyes downward to avoid his. I did not want to miss a word Paul said. Paul was giving testament to this small woman whose life gave forth tremendous goodness; I did not want my emotions to throw him. He began telling a story about her devotion to him, one of her grandsons:

"When I was a quarterback at Saginaw Valley State University, Nonna came to every single one of my games. My Dad picked her up and she drove to stadiums all over the state of Michigan with him…even to games that were at out-of-state colleges. She rode in the car, driving for hours, and stayed in a motel room with Dad. I thought to myself, 'Gosh, my grandmother is in her late-seventies, yet there she is sitting in the stands through heat, rain, snow, and frigid temperatures to see me play!' It made an indelible impact on me to know she was in the bleachers because of her love for me."

Paul moved the focus from him to Nonna's sphere of influence on her family and friends. "I think each person in this room would agree that Nonna was a positive, giving person. Every time you would greet her, every time you would talk to her, she would start with a big smile and little laugh."

I saw people nod heads in agreement and utter quiet chuckles.

"Nonna was very proud of her Italian heritage. One of the things I loved the most was to hear her tell stories of when she was a little girl in Italy. I loved hearing what the customs and traditions were: carrying the statue of the saint through the street on the Feast Day, the local chestnuts, the *formaggio* (cheese), and baking bread in the town's sole oven once a week.

Nonna was determined to pass the traditions to us. Each year she would have each one of us–from infants to grown-ups–take part in picking the grapes from her vines, crushing the grapes with grandpa's heavy grinder, and squeezing the pulp through the old press to extract the juice that was used for wine. Each Christmas, Nonna went through tremendous labor to carry on the tradition of the Southern Italian Christmas Eve seven fishes dishes. We all remember Nonna and Great-

Grandma at the stove on Christmas Eve frying the *grispelli*–it seemed likes hundreds of *grispelli*—for us.

Nonna's was happiest watching us eat the food she had prepared. Food was another way, in addition to the stories and traditions, that Nonna passed her heritage to us. She made sure there was a feast of traditional Italian foods for us every Sunday. She made so much food we would take home pots of it to savor throughout the week. She knew our favorites and would spoil us. Even when we were older she would surprise us–call us on the phone and ask us to stop by. On arriving we would find a roaster pan filled with *Steak Siciliano* or stuffed artichokes."

The nodding continued and laughter could be heard in-between Paul's descriptions.

"It is remarkable to recognize that the purpose of this woman's life was not any gain for herself; rather for selflessly making her family and friends happy. Hers was a life of sacrifice for those she loved. I'm not talking about 'sacrifice' as society views it today—an act begrudgingly performed. Rather Nonna's sacrifice was a life vocation to bring happiness to the ones she loved. That selfless service brought fulfillment and joy to her.

When I was in law school and my son, Ryan, was a baby, Nonna would call me on Sundays. 'You and Ryan come over. I know you are busy, so only stay for lunch if you want.' By the time Ryan and I got there Nonna would have some great pasta and Italian meat prepared. After stuffing myself with her delicious, homemade food, I would stretch out on her living room floor with a pillow from her couch under my head and the Sunday football game on the television. Nonna loved football and, even though in her eighties, always talked to me about the football team wins, losses, and rankings. She would sit with baby Ryan on her lap and watch the game. Being over-stuffed with food and exhausted from law school I was soon fast asleep on the floor. Little Ryan was pleased and content in Nonna's lap and would often fall asleep too. Nonna was blissfully happy we were with her because her life's devotion was her family. And for me there was rarely a more secure and loved feeling than being in Nonna's home, listening to her stories, both Ryan and I filled with her delicious food, and soundly asleep under her care."

Soft smiles remained on the guest's faces, sustained by the warmth recalled from stories of Nonna's tender love. Paul concluded.

"Nonna loved her family and lived a life of service devoted to her family."

Paul's eulogy described Nonna's legacy as *famiglia* (family), *tradizione* (tradition/heritage) and *amore* (love). To further Nonna's legacy my sister Laura carries on the *pane di pasqua* and traditional Italian recipes. My brothers Peter and Paul, along with their wives Nancy and Kim, continue the *vigilia di Natale* (Christmas Eve) tradition of seven fish dishes and frying *grispelli*, and thus further Nonna's legacy of love and devotion. We honor her emphasis on *la famiglia* gathering for a weekly Italian feast. In the year following her death we set a place for her at our huge family dinners to remind ourselves of the lesson she taught us about the significance of gathering to share family love, family joy, and family traditions, no matter what the distractions outside our dinner. At those gatherings, my father perpetuates the stories of heritage so that we never forget who we are and whence we came.

Paul's eulogy emphasized that Nonna loved her family and lived a life of service fostering the importance of family. That is part of her legacy and my family honors her love of family. Yet when I reflect I also see Nonna's legacy of courage: the lessons she taught me about living with obstacles. I look to her for courage—the courage that brings the determination, faith, conscience, virtues, strength, and hope to meet any obstacle head-on. Thus, for me to honor Nonna's legacy, is to live my life with courage: to base my actions in strong conscience, love, and kindness toward others, and to meet my challenges with faith, determination, strength, and hope. Using her life-lessons in courage I feel good about my actions no matter the outcome. Armed with that courage, you can bet I am going to live life with *gusto!*...no matter how many illnesses, how many surgeries, how much pain, how fatigued, or how many medications and side effects.

"*O mia bella Nonna.*" ("Oh, my beautiful grandmother.") I hear you whisper softly and determinedly, "*Coraggio, Leeza. Coraggio*". Although you may have passed from this world I whisper softly in reply, "*Tante grazie, Nonna.*" ("I thank you many times.") "Tante grazie" for those powerful words you spoke to me. "*Tante grazie*" for the lessons those words and your examples presented. Your courage brought peace, love, and joy to my life. Your lessons gave me the courage to bring peace, love, and joy to the end of your life. "*Dorme Bene, Bella Nonna.*"

It takes courage:

- To honor (bring peace, love, and joy to) the end-of-life.
- To cherish the legacy of a loved one after they have passed.
- To live a life of gusto...no matter how many obstacles get thrown in your path.

Epilogue

Five Lessons for Living from Italian Grandmother Nonna precede her *Lezioni Sei & Sette* (Lessons Six & Seven on the courage to grieve and to honor the end of life.

Be encouraged by Nonna's *Lezioni Uno–Cinque* (Lessons One – Five) in:

> *Lezioni Uno-Tre* (Lessons One–Three) *Coraggio! Lessons for Living from an Italian Grandmother Despite Illness, Pain and Loss.* 2009
>
> *Lezione Quattro* (Lesson Four) *Coraggio! Lessons for Living from an Italian Grandmother: Courage to Believe in Miracles.* 2010
>
> *Lezione Cinque* (Lesson Five): *Coraggio! Lessons for Living from an Italian Grandmother: Courage to Conquer Pain.* The courage to discover new perspectives and approaches to dealing with physical and emotional pain. 2012

www.WithCourageICan.com

Signing day for legislation recommended in the Michigan Commission on End of Life Care Report to Governor John Engler, January 3, 2001.

In hands of Governor Engler and author is House Bill 5062, newly enacted as Public Act 231 of 2001, the intent to eliminate barriers to prescribing medications for treatment of pain.

See story, Chapter 4.

Bibliography

Ad pushes Alternatives to Suicide, Traverse City Record-Eagle, November 14, 1998.

Angier, Natalie, *Diagnosis of Alzheimer's Is No Matter of Certainty, New York Times*, June 7, 1990.

Anti-B Group Running Ad Urging End-Of-Life Options, Gongwer Michigan Report, No. 220, November 13, 1998.

Assisted Suicide Still Lingering in Judiciary Committee, MIRS News, January 20, 1998.

Belkin, Lisa, *Doctor Tells of First Death Using His Suicide Device, New York Times*, June 6, 1990.

Bixio, Cesare Andrea, (music) and Cherubini, Bruno, (lyrics), *Mamma*,1940.

Brief Amici Curiae of Not Dead Yet and American Disabled for

Attendant Programs Today in Support of Petitioners, for Vacco v. Quill, Supreme Court of the United States, October Term, 1995.

Byock, Dr. Ira, *Dying Well, Peace and Possibility at the End of Life*, Riverhead Press, 1997.

Fein, Esther, B., *The Right to Suicide, Some Worry, Could Evolve Into a Duty to Die, New York Times*, April 7, 1996.

Gilbert, Marsha, *Panelists Call Assisted Suicide Murder, Not Help, Bay City Times*, May 19, 1995.

Governor Engler Executive Order 1999-4, as amended by *Executive Order 2000-2*.

House Bill 5474, Legislative Session 1997-1998. http://www.legislature.mi.gov/documents/1997-1998/billintroduced/House/htm/1998-HIB-5474.htm.

House Panel Debates Assisted-Suicide Bills, The Lansing State Journal, January 21, 1998.

Kevorkian Chronology, www.nightingalealliance.org/cgi-bin/home.pl?article=120.

Kubler-Ross, Elizabeth, *On Death and Dying*, Routledge Press,1969.

Kubler-Ross, Elizabeth, *On Grief and Grieving: Finding the Meaning of Grief through the Five Stages of Loss*, Simon & Schuster Ltd, 2005.

La Rosa, Julius, and Bleyer, Archie, *Eh, Cumpari*,1953.

Lifton, Robert J., *The Nazi Doctors*, Basic Books, Inc., 1986.

Michigan End of Life Commission Report
http://www.michigan.gov/mdch/0,1607,7-132-2940_3183-14145--,00.html.

Proposal B's Legacy Is Awareness, Lansing State Journal, November 9, 1998.

Schwarz, John Joseph, *No Escaping the Indignity of Death, The Detroit News*, September 1, 1997.

Senate Bill 200, Legislative Session 1997-1998, http://www.legislature.mi.gov/documents/1997-1998/publicact/htm/1998-PA-0296.htm.

Sides Take Stock after Proposal B's Defeat, Oakland Press, November 9, 1998.

Smith, Wesley, J., *Culture of Death*, Encounter Books, 2000.

Smith, Wesley, J., *Forced Exit*, Times Books, 1997.

Wallace Issues New Push to Legalize Assisted Suicide, MIRS News, January 14, 1998.

Wallace, Group Seek to Allow Assisted Suicide, Gongwer Michigan Report, January 14, 1998.

Weblink to Michigan Dignified Death Act, http://www.michigan.gov/documents/DignifiedDeathAct_69787_7.pdf

Weblink to Michigan End of Life Care, including resources, http://www.michigan.gov/mdch/0,1607,7-132-2940_3183_4895---,00.html.

Whitney, Gleaves, *John Engler: The Man, the Leader & the Legacy*, 2002.

Francesco Gigliotti (my Italian Grandfather-Nonno)
during a 1959 visit to his mother (pictured)
in his hometown of Motta Santa Lucia,
Provenzio Catanzaro, Italy.

See Story, Chapter 3.

Front cover: 50th Wedding Anniversary of Genaro and Giuseppina Rizzo, with daughter Saveria (my Italian Grandmother-Nonna) and Francesco (my Nonno), February 27, 1960.

Back Cover: Author's mother, Julia, in traditional Hungarian embroidered vest and costume. Written by her mother (my Hungarian grandmother-*Nagymama*) in German on back of photo:

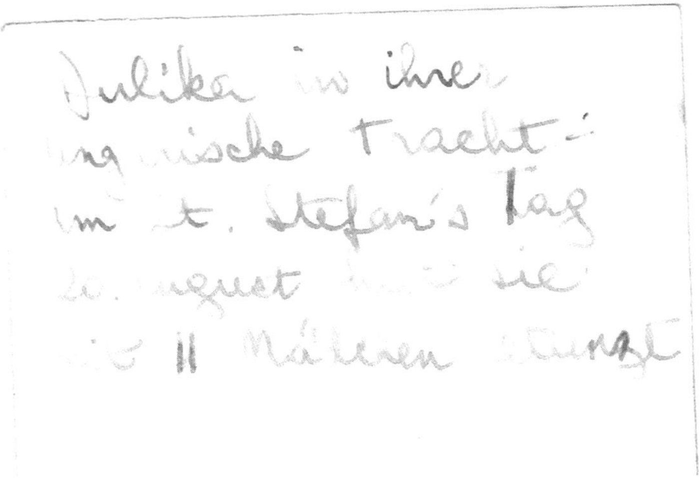

"Julia in her traditional Hungarian dress. On St. Stephen's Day, August 20, when she danced with 11 girls."

See Story, Chapter 3.